Road Signs on the High Road of Life

Road Signs on the High Road of Life

Lauren Ann Schieffer

Eloquent Books
Durham, Connecticut

© 2009 Lauren Ann Schieffer
All rights reserved. First edition 2009.

No part of this book may be reproduced or transmitted in any form or by any means, graphic, electronic, or mechanical, including photocopying, recording, taping, or by any information storage retrieval system, without the permission, in writing, from the publisher.

Eloquent Books
An imprint of Strategic Book Group
P. O. Box 333
Durham, CT 06422
http://www.StrategicBookGroup.com

ISBN: 978-1-60911-115-1

Book Design by Julius Kiskis

Printed in the United States of America
17 16 15 14 13 12 11 10 09   1 2 3 4 5

Dedication

This book is dedicated to my children, Melissa and Aaron, who are simply the whole world to me. I've had many jobs in my life, and yet from the moment each of them stirred within me my *vocation* has been these two miracles that God entrusted me with. My purpose in life is to lead by example and be the best model for walking the High Road I can be for them.

Contents

Foreword ix

Preface xi

Acknowledgments xiii

Introduction xv

Take the On-Ramp-Only Grounded Vehicles Permitted 1

Detour-Take the High Road 11

Fork in the Road-Choose Your Response 19

Welcome! You're Here by Choice 29

Fabrications Ahead-Tell the Truth, It's Always Easier 35

Caution! Uncomfortable Shoes Ahead 41

Attitude Pass-Only Positive Vehicles May Proceed 47

Rest Stop-Matters of Faith 57

Fuel Station-Prime the Pump 67

Success Junction-You Can Get There if You Put Your Mind to It. 75

Keep Driving-*Then* You Can Relax 83

No Road Rage Allowed 89

The Long and Winding Road 97

About the Author 105

Foreword

When I first met Lauren, I immediately knew she was a determined, hard working, goal-focused gal. She did not prove me wrong. In our working years together, she achieved just about every goal she set for herself. Two of her outstanding attributes were her oratory skills and her ability to express herself in writing. Many people can speak well, but not everyone has the courage or patience to transfer that skill to paper. I was surprised that she seemed not to have that realization, so I was thrilled when I found out she had written a book. I knew she could do it based on all the glorious letters she had written me, many that had me chuckling out loud!

With *Road Signs*, Lauren has not only written an amazing self-help book, but she takes you into her heart and spirit as she shapes some of life's most important lessons. It would be wonderful if young people would read this and take to heart what Lauren has learned and has to offer. It also would be wonderful if we, as human beings who deal and live with many people in our lifetime, would have a book such as this to read before we start our journey. We would understand others so much better and know why they do the things they do. However, we usually don't get the chance to have such a grand sweeping view and we are, therefore, left to work through many bumps in the road before it becomes smooth. Sometimes it never does smooth out simply because we don't understand them.

Thank you, Lauren, for opening your heart and for sharing the oh-so-many important lessons you have learned from your life's experiences. I know everyone who reads your story will thoroughly enjoy the trip.

Carolyn Ward
Independent Elite Executive Senior National Sales Director
Emeritus, Mary Kay Cosmetics, Inc.

Preface

On December 30, 2006, I lost one of the driving forces in my life – my dad. My father's death wasn't sudden as his health had been failing for some time. During the last six months of his life, I began to write his eulogy in anticipation of the day I would stand in front of other people who loved him, to honor his memory. What could I say about this 6'6" powerhouse of a man who was very human, very flawed, and yet still hung the sun and the moon for me? I began to think about everything my dad, "The Colonel," had taught me. I don't necessarily mean the academia or book smarts he offered. All of Dad's engineering wisdom and academic excellence went to my sister, who is brilliant. I was thinking more of the life lessons he instilled in me throughout my life – those lessons I find myself consistently imparting to my own children. That was the theme of my eulogy for my father, which became the seed of this book.

As the idea for the book continued to germinate, I realized I wanted to share more than just what The Colonel had given me. I also learned a great deal as I held my mother's hand through her battle with, and recovery from, alcoholism. My sister and I battled and recovered from eating disorders, and I survived the emotional and physical pains of assault. Other life lessons came from years inside the "pink bubble" of Mary Kay Cosmetics and the incredible, gracious lady herself, Mary Kay Ash. Some of my most valuable life lessons have come from my husband, Ron.

I was well on my way to writing this book when I became stalled. A little background – I am a tremendous fan of "Good Morning America" – almost to an obsessive level. I watched the inaugural episode and have watched just about every morning since then.

Most recently, I have built a profound admiration for co-anchor Robin Roberts. We are about the same age, have similar military backgrounds, values and outlooks on life. In addition, we both lost our dads at about the same moment in our lives. I have come to believe she is a soul sister who has just never met me. I'll fix that some day! Anyway, she had just published her book, *From the Heart, Seven Rules to Live By*. I bought it the day it became available and read it cover to cover that day. It was wonderful, but it also discouraged me. I thought, "Well, there it is. That is your book. It has been done well by someone else – a celebrity no less – so there is no need for you to keep writing yours." I stopped the project all together.

I realize now I was wrong to stop. Everyone's life lessons are unique and touch different people for different reasons. A pool of wisdom is a valuable thing. So I listened to my family and others close to me, and I finished my book. I hope you find it as valuable to read as I did to write.

Acknowledgments

First, above all, I give praise, honor and glory to my Heavenly Father who is the source of everything good in my life.

Sincerest gratitude goes out to my husband, Ron, who leads by example and walks the High Road every day. Not only that, but after 24 years together he still loves me. What a miracle. I am so grateful for him.

Love and hugs to Jan Moses, Sales Director with Mary Kay, who introduced me to the "pink bubble" and was loving, supportive and nurturing as I grew through the ranks with my Mary Kay business. She was equally loving, supportive and nurturing when I realized my life needed to take a different road and I narrowed that business down to a "personal use" level. She is a gem and for her lifelong friendship I am very grateful.

Thank you to Bob Potemski who taught me to be a better trainer and writer. Bob challenges me at every turn to be better than I am. He seems to see potential in me that I often can't see in myself. Even if he actually hasn't seen that potential, he always convinces me he has. Thank you, Bob.

To Linda Larson and Wanda McCallum, who read the initial, very rough manuscript and gave me invaluable feedback and recommendations. The finished tome is what it is because of your input. Thank you so much.

All my love and gratitude to my mother, Ruth Ann, and my sister, Christi, who never allow me to get too full of myself or wallow in my pity parties for too long. Thank you for always loving me as I am and "keeping it real" with me when no one else might.

Finally, I am tremendously grateful to The Colonel even though he is not here to accept that gratitude or read this book. The lessons my father taught me have been a consistent source of strength and wisdom on my life's journey. I truly wish I could have been a fly on the wall in Heaven when God and The Colonel sat down to hammer out who's *really* in charge.

Introduction

I grew up listening to folk music from artists like Jimmie Rodgers, Peter, Paul and Mary, and The Kingston Trio. Three or four of their albums were always stacked on my parent's record player. The comforting lyrics and rhythms became the background music of my childhood. Occasionally, I'll hear one of the old songs reproduced by another artist, and the lyrics come back to me instantly. One of the songs imbedded in my consciousness is a song titled "The Reverend Mr. Black" (Wheeler, Stoller, and Leiber). The refrain goes like this:

> *You've got to walk that lonesome valley.*
> *You've got to walk it by yourself.*
> *Oh, nobody else can walk it for you.*
> *You've got to walk it by yourself.*

From birth to death, we travel our own individual life road. We are growing – evolving into the people we are intended to be. Every human being walks their own road. I can't walk your road for you, and you can't walk my road for me. It is, indeed, a highway through a "lonesome valley."

Like any journey, the destination isn't always clear. With twists and turns aplenty, it's easy to get lost at the various crossroads we face. Luckily, road signs along the way guide us – if we are willing to read them. I believe the road signs on every person's road are identical. Which road signs you notice along the way depend entirely on what has happened to you in your life. Where you are in your life's journey and how focused you are on growth at that particular moment greatly affects the signs you see and how you acknowledge or act upon them.

Let me give you a few examples: If you are traveling on the highway and your car is on cruise control, you may not pay attention to the speed limit signs along the highway. They don't matter to you because you are maintaining a set speed. If you know you have 300 miles to go on the interstate before you reach your destination, you won't pay close attention to the exit signs for another 250 miles. If, however, nature calls, you will pay very close attention to those exit signs to find (and quick!) the amenities available at the next exit.

I was traveling on I-435 through Overland Park, Kansas, recently and noticed, for the first time, the brown sign that says, "Auto Route – Oregon Trail." I have lived in this city for six years, driven that particular stretch of highway hundreds of times, and I just now noticed that brown sign. I thought to myself, "Who cares about the Auto Route of the Oregon Trail?" Well, probably someone who is driving the path of the Oregon Trail for historical research or some other personal reason. My point is that it is up to each person which signs they notice, read and choose to follow because the signs are *identical* on all life roads.

What follows are some of the road signs that have guided me on my life's journey. These guideposts helped shape who I am and changed the course my life has taken. I admit I've had to learn some of these lessons a couple of times. Sometimes I took the same path multiple times before I actually saw the road sign and comprehended the lesson. I try to be honest and sincere about those times I've missed the road signs and been tripped up or driven off the shoulder of my life's road as a result. In the chapters ahead, I've tried to give you tangible tools that you can use to stay focused on these signs (or perhaps see them for the first time!).

INTRODUCTION   xvii

Take the On-Ramp – Only Grounded Vehicles Permitted
The foundation of all serenity is rooted in two pillars: self-esteem and respect to all people. Without these two pillars of serenity, you are just flapping around in the wind.

Detour – Take the High Road
Be the bigger person. Someone has to be – it might as well be you.

Fork in the Road – Choose Your Response
What happens to you in your life is not as important as how you choose to respond to what happens to you in your life.

Welcome! You're Here by Choice
For every choice, there is a result. Good results come from good choices, and bad results come from bad choices.

Fabrications Ahead – Tell the Truth, It's Always Easier
Telling the truth is easier, less stressful and requires less "gray matter" than being dishonest on any level.

Caution! Uncomfortable Shoes Ahead
There are three sides to every story: yours, mine and the truth.

Attitude Pass – Only Positive Vehicles May Proceed
A positive attitude is the single most important factor in any individual's success. You can do everything wrong with the right attitude and still succeed. You can do everything by the letter with a bad attitude and still go nowhere in life.

Rest Stop – Matters of Faith
Believing in something bigger than yourself allows you to release those things that are not in your control.

Fuel Station – Prime the Pump
You have to give before you get.

Success Junction – You Can Get There if You Put Your Mind to It
If you want something badly enough and are willing to work to achieve it, you can do anything.

Keep Driving – *Then* You Can Relax
Putting your priorities in order allows you to relax when the time comes.

No Road Rage Allowed
Being nice to people makes a difference. It enriches both your life and theirs.

The Long and Winding Road
Wrapping it all up for your journey.

I share these road signs, these life lessons, with the hope they may have a positive effect and ease your journey as you walk the highway through "that lonesome valley." Start walking!

Take the On-Ramp – Only Grounded Vehicles Permitted

God, grant me the serenity to accept
the things I cannot change,
the courage to change the things I can
and the wisdom to know the difference.

- Reinhold Niebuhr

Having lived all of my life in major metropolitan areas, I've had the opportunity to navigate highway construction zones many times – especially those involving freeway exchanges and improvements. I've watched the supports that will eventually hold spans of a freeway grow from a framework of wood, rebar and concrete. Each time I pass such a structure it provides me with a visual interpretation of what I call my "Two Pillars of Serenity."

Actually, whether I'm discussing effective communication, conflict management, or maintaining a positive attitude (or just about any other subject I might choose to open my mouth about), I find a way to tie in my two pillars because I think they are *that* important.

Getting back to my construction example, visualize yourself standing on two pillars with rebar encircling your legs, hips, knees and heels and extending into pillars of concrete. The rebar then continues through the concrete and into the ground. The pillars and rebar root you to the ground. They solidify your foundation so that when the winds of conflict, change and chaos blow, they blow around you but they don't blow you down. These pillars allow you to stay grounded regardless of the emotional traffic driving over you that might wear you down through the years. These pillars are *Your Self-Esteem* and *Respect to All People*.

Your Self-Esteem

Your first pillar is your own self-esteem. Understand, there is a difference between self-confidence and self-esteem. Self-confidence tells you that you can perform a task well. Self-confidence assures you that you are capable. *Self-esteem* tells you that you have value. You have value because you exist and are, therefore, worthy of merit. Self-esteem tells you that your value does not stem from who your parents are, who you are married to or dating, how much money you have or what your title is. Your value is not determined by what size you wear, what kind of car you drive, whose name is stitched into the collar of your clothes or what shoes you wear. Your value does not depend on the color of your skin, hair or eyes, or how fit, svelte or sexually attractive you are. None of these superficial things that society assigns value to matter at all. *Your value rests in the fact that you exist.*

Some people have that inherent value reinforced by their parents. They are the lucky ones. I have the privilege of knowing a few of them. Their solid self-esteem allows them to release what anyone says about them, thinks about them or does toward them because they are *solid* in their own value. That empowers them to do what is right because it's right, whether anyone is looking or not. What is especially impressive about these people is that their self-esteem comes hand in hand with humility. I admire them a great deal for that. Because knowing, in your core, that you have value – by your very existence – liberates you to be humble.

Take the On-Ramp-Only Grounded Vehicles Permitted

I've found that arrogance is really a sign of *low* self-esteem. I believe if you crack open the inner core of most boorish, belligerent, arrogant people, you will find a slush pool of low self-esteem.

Although I've held many jobs in my life, my current vocation is public speaking and corporate training. I love this work – it's my passion. In this role, I have the opportunity to travel all over the world, speaking and training. Before I began this particular phase of my life, I sat through many training sessions as a participant. I learned from each and every one of them, some of the lessons were intended by the trainer and some were *not*.

I remember a particular trainer quite well. She belabored the point of instructing participants to turn off their cell phones. She did not want them on vibrate because she could still hear them – she wanted them *off*. She expressed that texting under the table was unacceptable. She could see we were doing it and it was distracting. Whenever there was any sidebar chatter during her presentation as there often is in a corporate training environment, she stopped altogether and glared at the participants until they stopped talking. Or, worse yet, she called them out verbally about the chatter. The speaker was what many people might call brassy and aggressive in her behavior, and she consistently tried to impress upon her participants that they shouldn't take "anything from anyone." As a result, she lost half of the participants at lunchtime because they were offended at being treated like preschoolers.

A different session I attended was lead by two trainers. One was wonderful with the participants – funny and jovial. Toward the other trainer, however, she was exceptionally passive-aggressive and consistently sent verbal and emotional "zingers" to undermine the other's credibility with their participants. She veiled criticism and emotional abuse in the drippy sweet guise of "constructive input." I can only imagine the effect this had on the other trainer's confidence and serenity.

When I look back at both of these trainers, I suppose their behaviors were really a result of low self-esteem. I imagine the first had a fear of being taken advantage of and not being taken seriously. Maybe she has had to struggle, scrap and scratch for everything she has. Respect would, therefore, be very important to her and she might feel the need to demand it instead of earn it. The second trainer, on the other hand, solidified her own self-worth by belittling her partner trainer. The concept of rising above by pushing others down is, unfortunately, all too common. Being overly social with the participants increased her chances of receiving higher praise than her partner. This would allow her to convince herself that she must be a better trainer than her partner, thereby firming her sense of self-worth.

Unfortunately, few people are truly grounded in their own self-esteem from childhood. Many have to build it for themselves and must remain constantly vigilant to protect and maintain it.

A plethora of amazing resources are available to assist you in building and maintaining your own self-esteem. No one can do it for you. It is a uniquely individual effort for each of us. Let me share with you a few things that have been very helpful to me in my efforts on this front:

Keep a victory journal. Pick up an inexpensive spiral notebook. At the end of each day, write down something you did well that day. No scrimping allowed. There's never a day where you did *nothing* well. Once you get into that habit, begin to add one thing that is wonderful about yourself everyday. Again, no scrimping allowed – and no repeats of the previous day's entry are acceptable. This forces you to see things in yourself that deserve celebration. Be consistent in making your entries, and then look back over it after six to eight months. You will be amazed at how self-affirming it is (and how wonderful you are!).

Focus and build on your strengths. Each of us has gifts – things we do well naturally. It's very common to dismiss such things emotionally because we don't have to work on them. We tend to concentrate on the "problem areas" where we are weak. Don't get me wrong – I believe growth in certain areas is very important. I just believe we spend too much time focusing on areas that need improvement which can become very negative. I am a gifted speaker, performer and decorator. I am not a numbers person. I will never be able to do long division in my head, and that's okay. I can surround myself with people who are gifted in the areas that I'm not and utilize their strengths. It's a much better use of your emotional energy to acknowledge and build upon your gifts than it is to beat yourself up for things that are not your strengths.

Speak only positive things to yourself. I've found that one of the most important aspects of maintaining a solidly positive self-esteem is what you say when you talk to yourself. Notice I don't ask *if* you talk to yourself – we all do it! It is a sad reality that people often say to themselves things they wouldn't dream of saying to other people. I have to admit the first time someone told me to speak positive thoughts to myself or to write a personal affirmation, I said, "No thanks. I don't think so." It all sounded way too "Stuart Smalley" to me. Stuart Smalley was a character portrayed by Al Franken on "Saturday Night Live" in the 1980s. Stuart was a member of several 12-step programs. Throughout the day, he would look at himself in the mirror and say, "Because I'm good enough, I'm nice enough and gosh darn it, people like me." The concept of becoming like that made me want to throw up until I realized affirmations *do* work and they *don't* have to be nauseating. We just have to start where we are and write affirmations in small steps toward the self-esteem and confidence we wish to be true. Begin by finding a positive statement you believe in and feel good about and then grow from there. I believe what you speak about, you bring about. When we speak negative thoughts to ourselves, our subconscious believes it and sets about making it so. Start the self-esteem growth process here – with what you say when you talk to yourself. Speak only positive, nurturing thoughts to yourself.

A strong, solid sense of self-esteem is one pillar of serenity. However, if it is the only pillar that is solidly rooted, the other foot is free to run wild which could be dangerous. Picture yourself with one foot secured to the floor while the other foot works hard to get somewhere but can only run in circles. If the winds of adversity blow your direction, you can't escape them – because you are not rooted solidly enough to withstand them. The calamity may still throw you to and fro and eventually harm you. It is only with both pillars firmly rooted that you are grounded enough to withstand difficulty. Indeed, to carry the analogy one step further, items that are grounded solidly enough (ancient trees, buildings, mountains) cause the winds of adversity to go around them.

Respect to All People

Your second pillar is respect to all people. In his book, *How to Deal with Difficult People*, Paul Friedman frames this concept well with the simple sentence, "I will treat this person with respect whether or not I like what he or she thinks, says or does." I don't know if he intended that statement to be profound, but it was profound to me. In any given situation, I would choose to be treated with respect, and therefore will do nothing short of treating others with respect. Even if someone is not treating me with respect, I choose to treat them with respect. I don't want you to misunderstand my intent here. I am not asking you to respect all people. I certainly have met people who, because of their differing ethics or their behavior, I just can't respect. That doesn't mean I don't *treat them with respect*. It's a choice, and I choose to lead by example.

When our daughter, Melissa, was born, I was quite determined I would never use the words "bad girl!" There are no "bad girls" or "bad boys." Sometimes girls and boys choose to make bad decisions or exhibit bad behaviors. Yet as anyone who has parented a child through the "terrible twos" knows, such a commitment is put to the test on an almost daily basis. The first time it was truly tested, what ended up coming out of my mouth in a fit of frustration was, "That behavior is unacceptable in this household. This is NOT negotiable." This became the litany in our household. (Picture if you will; our three-year-old playacting with her doll propped up in the corner for "time out" and shaking her stubby little finger at it saying, "Dat b'havor is unceptable! Dis not go-shible!" It was at that moment we realized we might have taken the "no baby talk to the children" rule a little too far.) The point is I tried very hard to separate the behavior from the *child* so as to treat the child with respect while disciplining the *behavior*.

In the same vein, I strongly believe there aren't difficult people, only difficult behaviors. When you label someone as "difficult" it is counterproductive because it cripples your respect pillar. What the respect pillar allows you to do is to separate the person from the issue at hand. It allows you to address the problem and not the person. Some people choose to exhibit difficult behaviors. You have to be able to separate the behavior from the person so you can treat the person with respect. Even if they are not treating you with respect, treat them with respect.

If your respect pillar is solidly rooted, you can be secure in the knowledge your intentions were well meaning. Few, if any, people feel no guilt whatsoever when they mistreat someone else. When you disrespect someone else, you open yourself up to guilt – even at a subconscious level – which will ultimately rob you of your self-esteem.

We've all stumbled on this one, including me. I've slipped off the respect pillar and said or done something that demeaned or undermined someone else – intentionally and unintentionally. Guilt crept in like a sticky black ooze to coat everything I tried to accomplish afterward, and nothing subsequent was successful. The ooze quickly attacked my self-esteem pillar which then began to crumble and dissolve, and I was left with rubble. Only through admitting the mistake (again, whether intentional or unintentional), taking responsibility and apologizing did the black ooze recede and allow me to rebuild my pillars. Because of this, I learned the hard way that the easiest route -- the route that provides the most serenity and productivity in my life -- is the route highlighted by Paul Friedman: "I will treat this person with respect whether or not I like what they think, say or do."

Your two Pillars of Serenity function in harmony together like the computer operating system on your computer. Working in the background, they are the operating system for your life. When you're working on your computer, you aren't thinking about the fact you're working on Windows (or Linux, or Mac, etc.). You're surfing the web, typing a letter or creating a spreadsheet. If, however, the operating system on your computer crashes... nothing works. So it goes with the operating system for your life. Without your two pillars as the operating system working in the background, you can't withstand life's emotional power surges.

It's only with two secure pillars - your self-esteem confirming that

Take the On-Ramp-Only Grounded Vehicles Permitted 9

you have inherent value, and a commitment to treat all people with respect - that you can be grounded sufficiently. Without them, nothing else works.

Detour
– Take the High Road

"We must be the change we wish to see happen in the world."
- Mahatma Gandhi

While I was watching a beauty pageant several years ago, I heard something that inspired me. During the interview phase, the contestant said, "I set a bar for my life, and then I choose to live above it." I was thunderstruck. What a concept. I ran to grab a pen and a piece of paper so I could write it down before I forgot it. (I really wish I could remember which pageant it was – Miss America, Miss USA, Miss Universe, Miss Queen Princess of the World...I wish I could recall the contestant's name or her affiliation because I always like to give credit where it is due.) That concept is what it means to Walk the High Road: to set a bar for your behavior and your communication and then choose to function above that bar. I love that idea and have taken that as one of my life's principles.

Professional speaker and noted theologian Ivy Haley specifies in her book, *Discovering Your Purpose*, that in every culture there are universal principles – principles that just about everyone can agree upon. They might include honesty, integrity, kindness, and unconditional love. Putting these universal principles in the forefront of your "on-purpose" behaviors requires discipline. Haley goes on to say "some people mistakenly think that this perspective would put them at a disadvantage, but nothing could be further from the truth." I agree with her and take it one step further. I believe that principled, respectful behavior has to begin with me. This is what I call walking the High Road of Principle.

The High Road of Principle is always the most empowering and powerful road to be on. You never have to question your intentions, and you never have to metaphorically wash your feet off at the end of the day from wallowing in the muck and mire of bitterness, small thinking, spite and selfishness. Walking the High Road isn't always easy. I believe most people endeavor to walk the High Road. I say "endeavor" because everyone falls off now and then. We all have the "I blew it" days. We wash our feet off, climb back up on the High Road and try again. Some days we have one foot up on the High Road and one foot down in the muck, and we hope no one notices. We hope no one notices because sometimes it feels good to have one foot in the gutter. Sometimes it feels good to gossip about other people, to say spiteful things just to see the reaction you get, to bend or break the rules just to see how much you can get away with, or to expand a story in the telling. Yet, at the end of the day, we still have to look ourselves in the eye and wash that foot off before sliding it into our nice clean sheets.

I shared this concept once with a group of administrative assistants in New Jersey, and a young gal from the back of the room piped up with, "Why? Why is it always me that has to be the bigger person? I'm freakin' tired of being the bigger person." That garnered some empathic chuckles from around the room.

"Because you *can*," was my response. Walking the High Road of Principle is not always easy. It's a choice that has to be made every day. It's a commitment I make every morning when I look at myself in the mirror. I commit that today I will respect myself

Detour-Take the High Road

and others enough to step up onto and walk the High Road as best I can. I choose to lead by example.

During her sophomore year of high school, Melissa became embroiled in a social conflict. She was certain it would scar her for the rest of her life. The friend (we'll call her "Suzi") she'd been closest to for three years turned against her. Battle lines were drawn among the remainder of her friends, and emotional Hades ensued. This actually turned out to be one of the hardest challenges of my life as a parent. Staying out of it and allowing the necessary emotional growth to take its course was hard. Suzi had many tools working for her. She'd grown up in our little community, whereas Melissa was an import. Suzi had a true gift for sugary words and manipulation. Melissa was guileless, headstrong, stubborn and blunt.

Few teenagers maintain a solid sense of self-esteem to support them, and Melissa was no different. It is a difficult and often painful couple of years wherein we all decide what type of human being we choose to be. Suzi said, did and orchestrated some very hurtful things at Melissa's expense that fall. Every day, Mel came home from school agonizing or crying about the day's events and how she wanted to spit, lash back and emotionally rip Suzi to shreds. I knew I couldn't control Suzi's behavior. I also knew that as much as I wanted to fix the problem and take away the pain, I couldn't do that either. What I could have an impact on, though, were the lessons that Mel ultimately took away from the situation. I can't count how many times I repeated the phrase to Melissa, "Take the High Road, honey."

On one particularly difficult day, having repeated it to her yet one more time, Mel turned to me and said, "Mom, sometimes I want to take your 'High Road' and stuff it someplace very dark!" After overcoming my shock and suppressing a giggle I knew she would not appreciate, I took another tactic. "Melissa," I said, "your words are like toothpaste. Once you squeeze the toothpaste onto your toothbrush, you cannot put it back in the tube. It's the same with your words. Once they are out of your mouth, they are out – they're part of the great cosmic history for all time. This is why I keep telling you to walk the High Road and keep your mouth closed. Suzi has said many things to you and about you over the last month that I hope she will come to regret at some point in her life. Thus far, you have stayed on the High Road. Why would you choose now to stoop to her level and give yourself something to regret down the road? Why would you give *anyone* control over your toothpaste tube?"

In hindsight, I believe Mel was able to stay on the High Road -- for the most part anyway. Over time, the battle lines thinned and her friends recognized the true instigator of the strife. Suzi wandered off to find new friends, and Melissa remained content without Suzi in her life. I hope she took the lesson from the situation to heart so she doesn't have to learn that tough lesson again later on down the road.

Please don't construe this to mean that I was born walking the High Road. I've struggled with the natural human urge toward bitterness, small thinking, spite and selfishness just like everyone else.

For many years, I sang with one of the worship teams at my church. At that point in my life, I placed a great deal of my self-esteem in my performing abilities and often found myself frustrated being relegated to what I perceived as a background vocal. Our lead guitar player, Tom, was blessed with a truly amazing singing voice. Soft and clear, it seemed designed for folk, country, worship or just about any other style of music. Because of this natural ability, Tom most often took the lead

Detour-Take the High Road

vocal on any song we sang. Tom's teenage daughter, Monica, also sang with our group. During one particularly upsetting session for me, I expressed my frustration out loud. Easily within earshot of Monica, I said something about being tired of always singing backup. "It's like we should be called 'Tom and the Tom-ettes,'" I complained.

My comment was uncalled for. I said it hoping Monica would overhear and share what she heard with her father. Perhaps I expected him to apologize to me, give me a solo that should have been his, and then everyone would see me for the true talent I was. Needless to say, that didn't happen.

Instead, Tom stepped up on the High Road and ignored the comment. I'm sure he counseled Monica to do the same, but being young she wasn't equipped to slough off such a slight to her father. She shared her distress with the other vocalists and soon we had trauma, tension and chaos within the group. Although I was unwilling to admit it at the time, the fault was entirely mine. Slogging through the pettiness of jealousy and snippiness did not get me the result I desired. Had I taken my concerns to the group's director in a straightforward manner, he might have agreed and chosen music more suited for me to sing lead on. He might not have. He might have told me the structure of the vocal arrangements was exactly as he wanted it, but at least it would have prevented weeks of petty, emotional turmoil in the group. The ultimate result was that I left the group and robbed myself of the joy I felt from singing – even singing backup.

Even now, as enlightened as I think I am, I sometimes trip and slip off the High Road. Not long ago, my husband and I arranged to meet Melissa for lunch at a local eatery. We arrived before she did and waited for her outside the restaurant. A black pickup pulled up and parked in the handicapped spot right in front of the restaurant. I casually looked for the handicapped plate or a mirror tag, neither of which existed. A quite able-bodied man climbed out of the pickup truck and headed toward the door.

Ron made eye contact with the man and asked, "Are you handicapped?"

The man scoffed, tapped his head to indicate his brain and said, "Up here."

"Apparently," was my husband's response.

At that point, I started a slow burn. One of my greatest emotional stumbling blocks and quickest flash points is people who believe they are somehow more important than other people or more important than "the rules." Handicapped parking spots are reserved for people with disabilities for a reason, and I find few things as inconsiderate as able-bodied people using those spots. (I wish there were an immediate response number, like a parking control 9-1-1, for such an occasion that would send the police right away to promptly issue a grossly expensive ticket. But I digress.)

Melissa arrived and we walked into the restaurant just in time to run into the man walking out with his to-go order. I shot him *the glare*.

He flashed a cocky, sideways grin at me and said, "Thanks for watching my truck for me."

Slow burn met flash point and I called the man a name I choose not to repeat here. I don't use profanity; indeed I profess against using profanity in my training sessions. Therefore, hearing it come out of my mouth caught my husband and my daughter totally off guard. Unfortunately, I also attracted the attention of

Detour-Take the High Road

other restaurant patrons in the near vicinity. Yes, I had fallen completely off the High Road. I had stooped down to his level and gave him control of my toothpaste tube. And doing so did not get my desired result.

I presume with some certainty that the man did not drive away from the restaurant that day thinking, "You know my parking there really upset that woman. I was wrong and will not park in a handicapped spot again."

I've been asked by a colleague just what the High Road action would have been in that situation. I *could* have said nothing at all and realized there will always be people who try to skirt the rules. They eventually get "theirs" in some manner. I *could* have called the police immediately and hoped they arrived before he left. I *could* have written down his license plate number to give to the officer. I *could* have approached the man in a calm, assertive, controlled manner and explained to him why an able-bodied person parking in a handicapped spot is so offensive. Any of those options would have been a better choice. The result of my action was me having to metaphorically wash my feet off (and my mouth out!), apologize to my husband and daughter for my offensive language, and climb back up on the High Road. The climb that particular day was like climbing Mt. Everest for me.

Walking the High Road of Principle is a crucial choice that has to be made every day. Choice becomes discipline and discipline becomes habit. Some days we slip off. When that happens, the High Road action is to make amends, and to climb back up to try again another day. Set a bar for your life and choose to live above it. Rise above the morass of small thinking and petty actions to walk the High Road. It is the most empowering and most powerful road to be on.

Fork in the Road – Choose Response

Go ahead and hate your neighbor. Go ahead and cheat a friend.
Do it in the name of heaven. You can justify it in the end.
There won't be any trumpets blowin' come the judgment day.
On the bloody morning after – one tin soldier rides away.
                                    - Lambert and Potter

As I mentioned in my introduction, I have battled an eating disorder in my life. I am a recovering bulimic. I've been in recovery for decades, and the lessons I learned while climbing that difficult mountain are among the most valuable I've ever gained. One of the most memorable group sessions from treatment focused on the fundamental difference between reaction and response. Reaction happens on instinct. It is emotional and often visceral. Response requires *thought*, and that is the difference.

The facilitator opened the session with an intentionally controversial statement: "What happens to you in your life is not as important as how you choose to respond to what happens to you in your life." This was quite a firebrand, considering the audience was a group of recovering addicts. (I use the term "addict" inclusively. This particular group included recovering alcoholics, drug addicts and those, like me, with eating disorders. An eating disorder is an addiction that manifests itself with food, or the control of food, as its focus.) A healthy amount of discord and argument ensued over the facilitator's statement. The general theme of the argument came along the lines of a "my case is unique" defense.

One group member said, "That's easy for you to say, sitting there in the therapist's chair. You get to stand up and walk out of this group to your comfortable life. You don't have to live my life every day."

Another said, "Now wait one minute. I've had some pretty ugly things happen to me in my life, and they were important." I certainly could have been that group member. I've had some ugly, dark, scary moments in my life, too.

I'm the adult child of an alcoholic flower-child wannabe and a workaholic colonel in the Air Force. The Colonel and the hippie – how they ever ended up married I will never know. The marriage was difficult and tempestuous from start to finish. My sister, Christi, and I had no choice but to go along for the ride.

Throughout my childhood, I was taught (either by word or deed) that my entire value in life rested in either how svelte and sexually attractive I was, or in the accomplishment I could claim that was superior to anyone else's. I was a quick study. I learned that both attributes would be the best way to maximize my value as a human being. Not only could I be attractive and alluring, but I could be "super-kid" at the same time. As a child of the Air Force moving every three years or so, I learned very quickly that I had no control over any circumstance in my life. Military dependents are like leaves in a stream that go where they are told, when they are told, and do so with a "brave little soldier face." For that reason, I found it important to exercise any control I could. By age 13, I began practicing the cycle of

Fork in the Road-Choose Your Response

supposed control that is well known to bulimics: control over what came into and out of my body.

In high school, I continued being "super-kid" and added "caretaker" to my resume as I supported my mother through her cold-turkey recovery from alcoholism. I cooked and cleaned, in essence *functioned* for her when she couldn't seem to function, until she began to come out on top of the initial battle with the disease. I attended Alcoholics Anonymous meetings with her when no one else would, and began to learn the language and concepts of "the program" that would eventually save both her life and mine. (Mom has 30 years of sobriety under her belt this year. I'm so very proud of her.)

In college, Christi carried her "super-kid" persona to the extreme and graduated with a 4.0 in Chemical Engineering. Sometime during her senior year in college, my sophomore year, her veneer collapsed. Again, I played caretaker and held her hand through her breakdown and subsequent battle with anorexia and depression. I did laundry for her, delivered her homework to her classes, and picked up her next assignments for her when she couldn't deal with seeing people. I made sure she ate, and walked across campus in the middle of the night to be with her when she couldn't bear to be alone. (Christi also came out on the top end of that battle and continued on to earn a master's degree and doctorate in the same discipline. She is the smartest person I know.)

All this time, I was in belligerent denial of the cracks in my own foundation. When you are focusing on taking care of other people, it's easy to ignore your own issues. It was only during my senior year in college as I attended Al-Anon, which is therapy and after-care for family members of addicts, that I began to see I had a real problem of my own brewing.

I've never been petite. I'm a full-figured woman. Had I lived in the Renaissance era, I would have been the ideal picture of feminine beauty. In the late 1960s and early 1970s when Twiggy was in her fame, full-figured was the last thing I wanted to be. Even today, we are bombarded by the message that size of any kind is a horrible thing. Rail-thin women in Hollywood and on the fashion runway are considered the standard of beauty. It is a very difficult social environment for someone who is curvy.

When I was in junior high, my father passed by my bedroom as I was trying on some hand-me-downs from a neighbor. He stopped in the doorway as I was admiring a particular dress in the mirror and said, "Honey, when are you going to learn that those frilly little dresses just don't suit you? You are built like your father. You are built like a Mack truck, and frilly just doesn't work for you." I felt like I'd been *hit* by a Mack truck. My eyes welled up and I took off the dress. I never put it on again. I so desperately wanted to be petite, to be smaller than I was. Because of that experience, the size of the clothing I wore became all important. A size 6 became a type of Holy Grail to me. If I could just get into and maintain a size 6, I would be beautiful and everyone would love and accept me. The truth of the matter is that my bone structure with no flesh on it whatsoever would not fit into a size 6. I don't think I was a size 6 when I was six – much less a teenager. At that time, such common sense was of no importance to me. I vowed to do whatever it would take to achieve that all-important size 6.

And so I began a comfortable rhythm of binging and purging. I believed I was exercising "smart control" over my food retention. I was not, however, what I considered the average "binge and regurgitate" bulimic. I was not into throwing up. It made my stomach hurt. I knew it would damage my esophagus and corrode my teeth. I believed I was too smart for that. I had a better

Fork in the Road-Choose Your Response 23

solution. I would simply "accelerate my digestive system." I was merely "encouraging nature to take its course" more swiftly. I was abusing diuretics and laxatives. I could greedily stuff food into my system because I had the "smart" means of flushing it right back out. I didn't realize the damage I was doing to my digestive system. First and foremost, I was starving my body of nutrients because I was not allowing it to absorb the nutrients before I summarily flushed them out. Eventually that would lead to key system breakdowns that had to be rebuilt over time. Second, I was slowly destroying my digestive system's natural ability to process food. Because of the 10 or so years I spent pumping laxatives and accelerants through it, my digestive system forgot how to function on its own. I've now been in recovery for 24 years. Even now -- so many years later -- I have to be very careful with natural digestive coagulants such as bananas and bread. I've had several trips to urgent care over the years because of an impacted colon. I take fiber every day to keep the system functioning. Yeah, I thought I was exercising "smart control" over my food retention. I was so wrong. By trying to impose my control issues on my body, I disrupted its natural function forever.

In addition, I'm an assault survivor. I was assaulted not once, but twice.

While traveling in Greece the summer after my senior year in high school, I was assaulted on a beach on the island of Mykonos. I had stepped out of the hotel's discothèque to get some air on the private beach and to clear my head of the ouzo I was too young to have been drinking. I was approached by one of the men who lived at the hotel and functioned as waiter for our meals while we were there. He kept backing me farther and farther away from the hotel's discothèque and talking about "modern American women" who love foreign men. Before I knew it he was on top of me, pinning me to the sand. Someone from my group stepped out of the disco, and hearing me scream, came running down the beach to see what the problem was. This frightened the man enough to pull off of me and flee. I gathered up my torn clothes to cover myself and lied to the fellow from my group saying I was okay, that nothing really bad had happened. I was terrified that if I made a big deal about it, I would be sent home and the remainder of my study tour would be forfeited. Furthermore, I was sure that somehow it had been my fault for putting myself in a defenseless situation so late at night. I didn't tell any of the chaperones in charge and we left the following day for the mainland. My tattered clothing stayed behind in the hotel dumpster.

Four years later while driving home from a party after a theater rehearsal, my car broke down on the side of the Superstition Highway in Mesa, Arizona. It was 2:00 a.m. and I had been drinking a bit at a cast party. Even in September, Arizona heat is formidable, and I was minimally dressed in dance clothes. A car stopped to "help" but I soon found out that fixing my car was not on the assailant's mind. I found myself in the same position again. Common sense would have told me to run along the roadside where there was traffic, but I wasn't guided by common sense. I was driven by a profound shame at being the iron rod where lightning did indeed strike twice. I ran up the exit ramp and into a small wooded area to hide. Bad choice. Afterward, I was left alone to gather my clothes and wander back down to my car, which miraculously started. Once I got back to my apartment, I should have called 9-1-1. But again, I was crushed by a profound sense of shame. This was twice. It surely *must* have been my fault for being out at two o'clock in the morning, broken down on a freeway, wearing nothing but dance clothes and flip flops, with no contingency plan.

I never called the police. They would want to know things that

Fork in the Road-Choose Your Response 25

I, in fact, was already asking myself. "Why was I on the road so late with alcohol in my system, driving a vehicle on its last legs, and wearing nothing but a leotard?" "Why had I not gotten a license plate number or a good look at the man?" "What did I expect them to do about it now if I had nothing to give them to go on?" Instead, I called my father.

Dad was asleep when I called. His second wife answered the phone and refused to wake him. She and I didn't have a terrific relationship, and I certainly was not going to share my experience with her. She assured me she would have Dad call me in the morning. The next morning he left on a business trip without receiving my message. I sat alone in my apartment for two days, taking shower after shower after shower and not functioning – waiting for Dad to call and tell me what to do. When he did call two days later, he was furious with me for not calling the police. He was completely unequipped to deal with such emotional wreckage 500 miles away, so he did what he did best -- he kicked into survival mode. He recounted the story I had heard at least 100 times of when he had broken his nose playing college football and how he had stuck his fingers up the broken nostrils, set the cartilage himself, and gotten back in the game. He told me to get checked out by a doctor to make sure I was okay. I assured him that physically I was okay. "There is nothing to be done now, baby, but just move on" he said. "Set your nose and get back in the game." He determined my engine was fried from my description of how it had broken down, and he arranged for a rental car until I could get another vehicle. That was that. Life went on. And so did the shame – at least for a while.

I'm not sharing all of this with you to solicit sympathy or perpetuate any victim mentality. I truly released that long ago. Each person's path to recovery and subsequent release is unique. Mine involved some concentrated time beating the daylights out of a beanbag chair with a plastic baseball bat. I also had amazing counselors who loved me enough to tell me what I *needed* to hear rather than what I *wanted* to hear. As any recovering addict will tell you, recovery (be it from addiction or victimization) is a *process*, not a magic pill. My recovery was profoundly rooted in discovering my faith (or my faith discovering me) – a story I'll share with you later. That allowed me to discover my two pillars of serenity and cling to them with all the strength I had. Thankfully, sometimes I had people who loved me enough to duct-tape me to those pillars when I felt I couldn't hang on to them any more. I share this with you to offer empathy to anyone who might be feeling victimized by their life circumstances. Even though the hardest work of recovery is an inside job, no one recovers, releases and subsequently survives alone. It is always a group effort. Find a support structure – people who love you enough to be real with you whether you like it or not. Find people who will strap you to the two pillars of serenity and hold on with you when the winds of victimology blow.

Remember that belligerent group member bemoaning how important her life circumstances were? Yeah, it was me. In response, the facilitator nodded and agreed, "I'm sure they were important. They were not AS important as how you choose to respond to them. You have a choice. *Today*, you have a choice." She then continued to share with the group the fundamental difference between reaction and response. She tried to gently guide us to realize that, in our situations, to continue the cycle of reaction was to continue the cycle of being the victim and therefore, stunt our climb to victory over those circumstances. That concept was crucial to my recovery.

When Melissa was struggling through that rough year with Suzi, I continually encouraged her to take back her emotional control. Allowing yourself to wallow in any type of negativity because of

Fork in the Road-Choose Your Response

what someone else thinks, says, or does, puts them in control of your emotions – which ultimately gives them control over your vision, your goals, your productivity and your serenity. **No one should have control over those things but you.**

To continue reacting to any negative circumstance in your life allows the circumstance (the assailant, the bully, the passive-aggressive co-worker, etc.) to control you emotionally. I stopped reacting to my past a long time ago. I choose to not give those two assailants control over anything more than the few minutes of my life they took so long ago. That is all they will ever get from me. I stopped reacting to the outside pressures that sent me spiraling into bulimia by recognizing that my beauty has nothing to do with the size I wear. I take responsibility for my own actions and make my own choices. This gives me the sense of control I need.

Choosing response instead of reaction allows you to maintain emotional control, which protects your control over your vision, your goals, your productivity and your serenity. No one should have control over those things but you.

Welcome! You're Here by Choice

"Everything can be taken from a man but...the last of the human freedoms – to choose one's attitude in any given set of circumstances, to choose one's own way."

- Viktor Frankl

A second profoundly important group session I attended while in recovery focused on choices and the simple fact that *choices* manifest results. Good choices manifest good results. Bad choices manifest bad results. No special and favored human beings out there get to make choices without reaping the results. I believe sometimes the results don't come in this lifetime but the next – but there are always results.

I've made many choices that were good, as well as many that weren't so good. Every choice I've made has brought me to where I am today, and ultimately, I believe that's a good thing. Still, at some of the darkest and scariest moments in my life, I had to remind myself of the simple and yet powerful wisdom I learned in recovery. We are where we are based on the choices we've made.

After my mother and father divorced, Mom married J.R. He was such a character – fun, witty, goofy and capable at the same time. J.R. was like a cross between Cary Grant and the Marlboro Man – rough and carefree, smooth and spontaneous. I was crazy about him. J.R. made a choice early in his life to smoke. He made a second choice later, after he married my mother and she had quit smoking, to continue to smoke. Both decisions set up the ticking time bomb inside his body that is all too familiar to doctors and their patients who smoke. The initial result was bone cancer that forced him to sacrifice most of his jaw bone and his salivary glands. The secondary result was a futile battle with emphysema – one that he couldn't win.

J.R. was also a recovering alcoholic. He struggled with the demons of the disease as many recovering addicts do. One day, he just disappeared. No note, no phone call – just no J.R. He was gone for about a week and a half. My mother was frantic. A hundred horrible scenarios played out in her head. Ten days later, he strolled in casually at dinner time with something behind his back. After the initial relief at his safety and welfare, Mom lit into him like a Roman candle. With a mischievous grin on his face, he sheepishly pulled a beautiful potted orchid from behind his back and said, "I went to find you an orchid. It had to be perfec,t and they only grow this particular orchid in Brazil." Total silence. My sister and I squirmed a bit as his words just hung in the air. Mom didn't say another word. She just turned around, served him up a plate and we ate dinner in silence. Who knows where he actually was during those 10 days, but the result of his choice was a fundamental crack in the trust my mother had in him.

This lead to a brief separation during which J.R. made yet another choice that would bring about the final straw result. That choice was to be unfaithful. It wasn't until several years later, long after he and Mom had reconciled, that the results of these choices would come crashing down on J.R. and our family. It was incredibly difficult for my mother (and her two daughters) to watch helplessly as J.R. succumbed to bone cancer,

Welcome! You're Here by Choice

emphysema and ultimately, HIV. The perfect storm of terminal illness hit him and took him away within one year. I watched my mother rail in grief and anger at him for his poor choices, while lovingly tending to him before he passed away. Choices manifest results.

I was driving home from training in a small town in Kansas not long ago, and my rental car alerted me that my fuel was low. My GPS unit indicated there was a gas station seven miles ahead and that I should take the next exit. (I now know that the GPS unit was indicating seven miles as the crow flies...) The next exit took me off on a gravel road, which led to a dirt road, which led to a cow path, which led to a squirrel run...and I realized I was in a real fuel predicament. I was reaping the result of choosing *not* to fill up in the small Kansas town before I left for home. I was weary from training all day. It was pouring rain and I was eager to get back home. The miles-to-empty display on the rental car indicated that I had enough fuel to make it home. I knew I had to top off the tank before I turned in the rental car so I figured I'd just fill it once. (Lesson learned: The miles to empty indicator is really only an estimation.) So there I was, in the pouring rain, driving down what could be called a path at best. (The GPS unit couldn't even name it – it simply said, "Continue on road.")I was stressed out and praying that I didn't run out of gas in the middle of nowhere. Had I made a different choice up front, I would not have had to face the possibility of being stranded. I could have avoided all the added stress at the end of a long day. I took stock of the situation at that point and reminded myself, "We are where we are based upon the choices we have made." Fortunately, the squirrel path eventually led to a county road instead of up a tree, and I was able to coast into a gas station just as the car started sputtering.

Right out of high school, my husband attended a vocational

technical school rather than a four year university. Even though that choice was pretty much made for him by his family, it was still a choice. He graduated with a technical degree and immediately went to work in the field. Throughout our marriage, we have had some lively discussions about the value of a four year college degree compared to a vocational degree. It really hadn't made a whit of difference in our lives, he argued, so what was the big deal? The result of the choice that had been made for him so many years ago manifested itself recently when we moved to the Heartland of America.

Ron had 20 years of experience in telecommunications and had earned a position as "Member of the Technical Staff" through hard work and being an exemplary employee. We naturally assumed he would easily find a job in his field in Kansas. But without a four-year degree in engineering, Ron found it very difficult to find that job. For months, he loaded trucks for UPS at night and delivered flowers during the day to help us stay afloat while he pounded the pavement looking for "a real job." He was eventually contacted by a stable and growing company that needed someone to test their software, which is Ron's tour de force. He has been gainfully employed ever since. But Ron was forced to do what many men in his position would have refused to do. He swallowed a great deal of pride and started at entry level – at half what he had been earning before. Now he is the one preaching to our children about the necessity of at least a four year degree in today's workforce. He is encouraging them to make a different choice than the one that was made for him.

I made a decision a year and a half ago to finally buckle down and bring our family out of credit card debt. We had built up considerable debt over the years and it was weighing heavily on me. I made a choice that every spare dollar I had would go toward the debt. Because of that choice, I was able to pay off

Welcome! You're Here by Choice

the credit cards in roughly 13 months. That was the good result. As an independent contractor, I don't have traditional employee income wherein a company takes my taxes out of my paycheck automatically. I'm responsible for paying my own taxes quarterly. The choice I made was to pay off the credit cards instead of paying my taxes. Enter the bad result.

The bad result was being faced with a sizable payment due to the Internal Revenue Service the next year, which I needed to pay off in installments (plus interest and penalties). I still believe it was a good choice in general: $20,000 of high interest credit card debt vs. $6,000 to the IRS. In hindsight, however, I could have made yet a *different* choice. I could have paid the taxes quarterly and taken two years to pay off the credit card debt. The result of the choice I made was that I needed to pay my quarterly taxes as well as unpaid taxes from the previous year. That meant my income was cut by a third while I was trying to pay college tuition for my daughter in an incredibly difficult economy. Each time I felt frustrated because we didn't have extra funds for dinner and a movie, I reminded myself, "We are where we are based upon the choices we have made."

While I've highlighted these few negative instances to make a point, it is important to remember that good choices manifest good results. I don't encourage you to focus only on bad choices you might have made. Focus on the good choices, so you can continue to make good ones. I believe very strongly that you get what you focus on. Don't spend too much time dwelling on your mistakes. Take the lessons from your poor choices and move forward to make better choices. Focus heavily on the good choices you have made so you can repeat them again and again for continued excellent results.

Fabrications Ahead – Tell the Truth, It's Always Easier

"The best ammunition against lies is the truth."
― Ernest Hemingway

I've discovered in the most recent years of my life that telling the truth is easier and creates less stress. I say "in the most recent years" because for a good number of years, I was a practiced liar. It is a symptom and natural part of addiction. All addicts, at some level, are practiced liars.

I could say I came by it naturally (and to a certain extent I did because addiction is hereditary). I watched my mother lie about whether or not she'd been drinking, where she'd been, and what she'd been doing. I watched my father lie about his philandering. Come to think of it, I don't think that my parents were ever truthful with each other.

Fabrication, exaggeration and facades were part and parcel in our home. Mom regularly fabricated a different picture of our lives to temper the edge of her own mother's disapproval.

The morning after one particularly wild, drunken blow-out party my parents hosted, my mom barreled into our bedroom. "Get up! GET UP! We've got work to do!" she hollered as she dragged us out of bed.

"Geez, Mom, where's the fire?"

"Grandmother just called. She's on her way over."

We knew what that meant and it was *not* good.

The house, the bedrooms and the yard were trashed with dishes, discarded bottles, cups and napkins. Mom was terrified to let her mother see the house in its current state of chaos. Rather than being honest – that they had hosted a party the night before and had yet to clean up – Mom flew into frenzied activity. We were expected not only to help, but to match her manic pace. We gathered up all the dirty dishes and shoved them under beds or in the dryer. We stuffed the trash into any bag, box or container we could easily lay hands on and shoved it all into the alley. There was no time to vacuum, so we simply raked the shag carpet instead. We wiped down all visible surfaces and blew frantically at dust that had nothing to do with the previous night's festivities.

Finally with a quick spit-polish on ourselves, Christi and I looked like we'd been up for hours instead of 30 minutes.

I don't remember Grandmother's visit at all, only the cyclone of activity before and the exhaustion after. Mom was spent. Creating the façade for her mother had taken everything out of her. I don't think we retrieved the dishes from their hiding places for days.

My sister and I followed in those footsteps. To mask the dysfunction of our home, Christi and I regularly fabricated stories. It seemed creating *any* reality other than our own was a better choice. So we lied -- regularly.

Fabrications Ahead-Tell the Truth, It's Always Easier

In junior high and high school, I was never sure what state Mom would be in when I came home, and it was just too socially dangerous to invite friends to come home with me. I got into the habit of saying Mom had cancer and was too ill for me to have any friends over. That solicited sympathetic offers of assistance from well-meaning friends and their parents, which then needed to be rebuffed with further lies – and the cycle continued. I even fabricated two additional siblings – twin sisters, Cori and Tori. I don't remember the purpose these phantom sisters were supposed to serve. Once created though, I had to perpetuate the story. I *do* remember the moment when that particular lie was discovered.

My best friend at the time, the one I cared about more than anyone, was flipping through a memory album and came upon a newspaper clipping about my mom earning her private pilot's license. The clipping listed mom's two (not *four*) daughters, Christi and Lauren. Holding the clipping, my friend looked me in the eye and said, "Cori and Tori, do they exist?" Anyone who has been discovered in a lie knows the leaden feeling I got in the pit of my stomach. I swallowed hard and told her the truth. Then I began sharing my reality with her. I fully expected her to never speak to me again. Rather than driving her away as I expected however, she forgave me and it made us closer. She became a rock for me amid the sea of dysfunction that was my life at the time. A wise woman would have learned from that moment, but I was not yet capable of wisdom.

It might be easy to blame my lying on genetics, but that would discount my own responsibility. Every person makes a choice as to whether they are going to be a truthful person or a deceitful person. I made the wrong choice for way too long. Plato said "false words are not only evil in themselves, but they infect the soul with evil." I believe that is true because between my sister's graduation from college and my initial recovery from bulimia, lying became entirely too easy for me. I was on my own with no one to answer to. No one knew the truth (whatever the truth was), so no one could look me in the eye and confront me with it. I lied to cover up my eating disorder. I lied to boyfriends who thought we were exclusive – when in fact I wasn't – which ruined many relationships. There were big lies, small lies, lies of exaggeration, and lies of omission. It was easy and commonplace. I was not at all someone that could be trusted. I was an accomplished liar.

A mirror was put to my face with regard to this in my very first group recovery session. The facilitator quoted Adolf Hitler, "Make the lie big, make it simple, keep saying it, and eventually they will believe it." I was outraged. I was incensed that she would have the audacity to equate me with Adolf Hitler. She also quoted Franklin D. Roosevelt, "Repetition does not transform a lie into a truth," and Baltasar Gracian, "A single lie destroys a whole reputation for integrity." She loved her quotes (as do I) and had them for just about any subject we would cover in group. She printed each one on a 3x5 card for me and instructed me to keep the card with me and read it once each waking hour for a week. The wisdom of what she was trying to hammer into me did not sink in for some time.

The importance of truthfulness finally began to make sense to me in a subsequent session about trust. I said I didn't trust anyone because no one had ever proved they were trustworthy to me. She asked me, "Lauren, isn't it more truthful to say that you have never proved yourself trustworthy?" Then she handed me the 3x5 that really made the difference: George Bernard Shaw, "The liar's punishment is not in the least that he is not believed, but that he cannot believe anyone else."

It wasn't until I had a few years of recovery under my belt that I realized the truth is easier. When you tell a lie (big or small),

Fabrications Ahead-Tell the Truth, It's Always Easier

you always carry the burden of remembering what you told to whom. Lies grow and propagate other lies, which then require more memory space in your brain. Inevitably, the memory cells fill to capacity and begin to leak. At the risk of throwing another quotation out here, this is one of my favorites: Ronald Reagan, "I'm not smart enough to lie." At this point in my life, that is so true. I just don't have enough space in my brain to carry even one fabricated story, much less multiple ones.

As is the case with all parents, I've tried hard to "save" my children from the mistakes I've made. This lesson about lying has been one of the hardest learned for me and therefore, one I've tried the hardest to instill in my children. All kids lie. They lie to save themselves from repercussions for their errors or behavior. They lie to avoid doing their homework. As they become teenagers, they lie to keep their parents in the dark about their lives. They experiment with things their parents wouldn't approve of, and then they deny it. Kids lie.

My son, Aaron, struggled quite a bit with this. I think the fear of disappointing his parents was his primary motivation for not being truthful. With regard to schoolwork or chores, he consistently told us what he thought we wanted to hear rather than the truth. It took a while for him to realize that the disappointment eventually came and was, in fact, much greater when the facts actually came out.

The old adage about parents having eyes in the backs of their heads likely stems from parents having lived longer and probably having done most of what their own kids are lying about. I consistently caught my kids trying to pull one over on me. Each time it happened, I reminded them the greater of the two offenses is the lie. The German philosopher, Friedrich Nietzsche said, "I'm not upset that you lied to me. I'm upset that from now on I can't believe you." Each time they were caught in a lie, my kids had to rebuild my trust again from square one.

For our family, it's been a slow and strenuous learning process, and yet I think we've come out on top. I believe my kids finally get that telling the truth is easier. You see, the truth never changes, and therefore, it doesn't require as much effort. Furthermore, the truth doesn't have to adapt to serve the purpose of the liar. The truth just is.

Tell the truth, regardless of the perceived consequences. It's simply easier and will always benefit you in the long run.

Caution! Uncomfortable Shoes Ahead

Well, I've got a hammer and I've got a bell and
I've got a song to sing all over this land
It's the hammer of justice
It's the bell of freedom
It's a song about love between my brothers and my sisters
All over this land.

- Seeger and Hays

On one particularly memorable day for me, I came home from high school with a friend in tow to find my mother inebriated beyond reason. I was so embarrassed by her behavior that I couldn't think straight. I tried to hurry my friend back out of the house and turned my back on my mother as she slurred some perceived explanation to me.

She shoved her way past me to confront my friend. "You see?" she slobbered. "You see what I have to put up with from this ungrateful child?" My tolerance snapped. Emotionally, I blew a circuit.

"Mom, you are a *drunk*," I cried. "You're an alcoholic. Dad knows it. Christi knows it. I know it. You had better start believing it because I was your last support in this house and I am through. I'm not cleaning up after you and your messes anymore."

She looked at me like I had slapped her in the face, and said, "Walk a mile in *my* moccasins, kid, and see how it feels."

This was something she said quite often, and therefore it had very little impact on me at the time. What did impact me was her subsequent telephone call that same day to Alcoholics Anonymous. I went with her to that very first meeting and watched her struggle to put her feet on a different road: a sober road.

While it was easy for me to dismiss her statement at the time, I realize now there was wisdom in it. The sentiment is rooted in an old Hopi Indian adage, that one can't truly know a man until he has walked a mile in that man's moccasins.

I've learned in my life's journey that there are three sides to every story: yours, mine and the truth. We all view life, love, conflict, work, justice and faith from our own paradigms. Our perceptions are shaped by our own unique, personal journeys. I can't ever truly see things from your perspective, and you can never truly see things from mine. Be that as it may, I can try to put myself in your shoes long enough to *empathize* with your position.

According to wordnet at Princeton.edu, empathy is "the capability to share your feelings and understand another's emotions and feelings. It is often characterized as the ability to 'put oneself into another's shoes.'" Empathy, therefore, comes from a commonality – a oneness. Empathy involves the ability to understand how a person feels based upon a similar experience. While I may have never placed my hand on a hot stove and received third degree burns on my hand as a result, I have tripped and fallen against the furnace in our home and received third degree burns on my arm. I can, therefore, say, "I know how that feels." I may not have watched my spouse waste away and succumb to the ravages of cancer, but I have watched my father slip away into the black hole

Caution! Uncomfortable Shoes Ahead

that is Alzheimer's. I know the sickening feeling of helplessness and the sad sense of loss. I can, therefore, empathize.

It might be easy for a busy executive to look at someone standing on a street corner with a sign that says, "Homeless and jobless – please help," and think to himself, "Geez, go get a job, would ya? No one gave me any handouts. I work hard for what I have." At the same time, the vagrant might look at the executive as he walks by and say to himself, "Life must be pretty easy for you, buddy. You have a perfect home, perfect family who loves you -- no worries at all – and you can't spare a buck or two so I have something to eat tonight?"

The *truth* is undoubtedly somewhere in the middle. There are three sides to every story.

In 1997, my family took a vacation driving in a large loop across 12 states. We spent two weeks piled inside the land-yacht that was our Cadillac driving no more than 300 miles in a day. We stopped to see anything and everything we wanted to see. It was one of the most wonderful and memorable experiences we have had as a family. One of the stops we made during that trip was outside Rapid City, South Dakota. We visited Mount Rushmore because the kids and I had never seen it. It's a tremendous sight – a true engineering and artistic marvel. The visitor's center piped patriotic music behind us as we made our way along the American flag-lined path to the viewing platform. This national monument accomplished exactly what it was supposed to do: stir raw emotions of patriotism in the hearts of Americans.

The next day we visited a different monument, one that was being forged out of a mountainside to honor the Ogala Lakota Sioux Chief Crazy Horse. A tour of *that* visitor's center left me with a very different feeling.

My first impression was something along the lines of, "Gee, they haven't gotten very far with this thing, have they?" Then I read the information in their visitor's center noting the project has resolutely rejected federal funding that might have moved the monument along at a faster pace. They have steadfastly rejected assistance from a government that, as they see it, has never kept a single promise it has made to the Sioux Nation. Reading the story of Crazy Horse and the nation he represented, I got a very different sense of the history so stirringly chronicled just a few miles away at Mount Rushmore.

As we left the Rapid City area and headed east across the Badlands of South Dakota, I was deeply troubled by the dichotomy of our history. I thought, "Walk a mile in their moccasins, Lauren." If some nation or group of people decided today, in the 21st century, that America was a land of promise and wealth, and they were going to take that land for their own – by force – we would fight to the death to defend our homes and families. The thought of someone walking into my home and saying it was theirs now simply because they wanted it and had the force to take it is absolutely absurd in today's reality. Yet that is exactly what happened on this continent some 200 years ago. The English settlers, the French settlers and the Spanish settlers (as well as Germans, Italians, Dutch, and so on...) carved out pieces of this continent with no regard for the sovereign nations that were already here.

As I contemplated that, I was struck with the futility of any empathy I might pretend to feel for Native Americans – within the context of *my* life. I firmly believe that what happened to the Native Americans, the indigenous people of this continent, was wrong. As a country, we would not stand for such a thing today. It was wrong. On the other hand, if someone were to come to me and say, "You are right.

Caution! Uncomfortable Shoes Ahead 45

It was wrong. We're going to give it all back to the Native Americans, so pack your things and get out," I would say, "Oh, I don't think so. This is *my* home." Interesting predicament, huh? This was their home first. This is my home now. There are three sides to every story: yours, mine and the truth.

As I speak, teach and train, I try very hard to impress this "three sides" mentality. I try to play "devil's advocate" for people. Invariably as I am speaking on conflict management or how to communicate with difficult people, one of my participants will bring up a situation that is seemingly insurmountable to them. They are usually looking for me to tell them they are right and the other person is wrong. I rarely give that to them – that is not my job. My job is to encourage them into the other person's moccasins for a moment. I try to help expand their thinking a bit. I ask them things like, "What do you think 'Barbie' was feeling at that moment?" "What do you think 'Barbie' might be afraid of that would cause her to behave that way?" "Think back, honestly. What do you think you could have done or said differently that would have avoided this situation from the beginning?" Sometimes this "three sides" approach is met with insightful reflection. Sometimes it's not, but that doesn't make it any less necessary. Only after walking in 'Barbie's' shoes can the participant build the empathy necessary to resolve the situation with honesty and respect. Only then can this person step up on the High Road and begin finding common ground.

I believe this is the optimum strategy in any conflict situation: finding common ground. In every conflict you face, ask yourself, "What can we agree on?" I might encourage the participant to go to 'Barbie' and open a dialog based on that premise. "Can we agree that we each want to have a comfortable working environment that is free from conflict and drama? Good. What else can we agree on?" Begin constructing a bridge to resolution on that common ground. Sometimes you have to begin this process quite broadly. "Can we agree that we will each leave this room without killing the other? Good! What else can we agree on?"

Walking the High Road usually involves giving before you get, so establish ground rules for a respectful dialog and begin by asking the other person how they perceive the situation. Allow them to share their insights and their perceptions. You might need to physically bite your tongue to prevent yourself from throwing in a "yes, but..." Allow them to vent until they have clearly expressed their side of the situation, then you can respectfully share your side. Together, you can begin searching for where the truth lies – usually somewhere in the middle. Seek out those nuggets of commonality you both can buy into. Slowly, pylon by emotional pylon, build the bridge on each and every scrap of common ground you can find.

I recognize that sometimes you begin building a bridge on common ground and find the two sides can't meet in the middle. That is when you agree to disagree and treat each other with respect anyway. I believe that last clause to be profoundly important: *treat each other with respect anyway*. In today's society, the concept of "agreeing to disagree" has become a bit patronizing. It is all too easy to pretend to "agree to disagree" and still remain divisive and condescending. Agree to disagree AND treat each other with respect anyway.

If my theory is correct and there are three sides to every story, then the only way to really empathize with the other person and get at the truth of the matter is to walk for awhile in their moccasins. It's not always a comfortable journey, but it's always the right place to start.

Attitude Pass – Only Positive Vehicles May Proceed

When you're smiling
When you're smiling
The whole world smiles with you
When you're laughing
Oh, when you're laughing
The sun comes shining through

But when you're crying
You bring on the rain
So stop your sighing
Be happy again
Keep on smiling
'cause when you're smiling
The whole world smiles with you

— Shay, Fisher, and Goodwin

Every cloud has a silver lining, but actually seeing that silver lining is a choice. When I began my business with Mary Kay Cosmetics and was supporting my portion of the household budget with my sales and recruiting efforts, I often came home from a skin care class late at night and Ron would ask how it went.

"Not great. I only sold $19," I might reply.

To which my husband would say, "Hey, that's $19 you didn't have before you left this evening."

I focused on being $106 short of the $125 goal I'd established for myself. Ron focused on the fact I was $19 richer than when I left.

His attitude was a little more positive than mine!

When you can't immediately see the silver lining, create one. Ron has a characteristic phrase that works when nothing else will – "That beats a poke in the eye with a sharp stick!" Now, I don't know if he was consistently threatened with sharp sticks as a child or what, but in his book anything and everything beats a poke in the eye with one. Therefore, in Ron's opinion, anything that is not a poke in the eye with a sharp stick is a silver lining.

Mary Kay Ash used to say, "Your attitude determines your altitude." I'm not at all sure that quote originated with Mary Kay although she certainly made it a standard for her sales force. It is, I believe, a certainty. I've never met, nor have I ever heard of, anyone that is wildly successful with a consistently negative attitude. Your attitude, whether positive or negative, is always "leaking" out of you in some way. The question to ask yourself is: "What am I leaking? Is it fresh, positive and fragrant? Or is it stale, negative and skunky?" The reality is you can do everything wrong with a positive attitude and still succeed. You can do everything perfect to policy with a stinky attitude and still get nowhere.

We have all met people who can light up a room just by walking in. As I travel and speak, I see it consistently. These positive people come into the conference room and others smile, wave, and offer up the seat next to them.

We have also encountered people who suck the very light and life from the room. These people are great black holes of negativity consuming any and all optimism in their wake. As these people enter a room, they are spotted peripherally and suddenly everyone else becomes profoundly focused on their conference agenda or workbook. I see them casually pick up their purse, coat or briefcase, and set it on the seat next to them to indicate that seat is "unavailable."

You cannot be impacted by, or have an impact on, people that refuse to be around you.

In my years as a Mary Kay sales director, I was extremely fortunate to be surrounded by inherently positive people. Predominately this was by choice, although some of it, I'm sure, was by the law of natural magnetism. Positive people attract other positive people. Even so, in Mary Kay as in any microcosm of human society, you will find negative people sprinkled in with the positive.

I saw it consistently when I trained consultants at local or regional events. Consultants would approach me afterward with questions. What I had shared with them was all well and good, but it wouldn't work for them because they had this going against them or that burden to bear. This situation was stacked against them, or that consultant or director had done them wrong. I would listen to the whole story. Then I would say something to the effect of, "I can imagine that was very frustrating for you. Tell me what you are doing to rise above it." "What positive steps have you taken to move past this and put it behind you?" Or, "Who do you think is responsible for creating the light at the end of the tunnel you seem to be in right now?" Most often, this was met with an attempt to reiterate the challenge, obstacle or perceived slight as they thought I obviously had not fully understood their unique situation or the gravity of their woe. That's when I would gently interrupt them with something like, "Hold on a minute. I think I have a grasp of your situation. I know how you feel. I've felt that way myself a time or two in my career. I've found the answer is always between my own ears. I know you will look back on this time in your career as one of your greatest growth opportunities. Here is my business card. When you have a specific plan in place for turning this stumbling block into a stepping stone, I want you to e-mail me with that plan. I will be so excited to cheer you on, and I will have a special gift for you to celebrate your success." I felt fairly confident in saying this because only about 1 in 100 of those Eeyores ever actually made the effort to move out of their current quagmire. Like the donkey character created by A.A. Milne, these negative people consistently see the cloud within the silver lining. When I did hear from one of them, the gift I sent them, along with an encouraging word, was always a pack of note cards they could use in their business. The note cards were imprinted with the quote, "Your attitude determines your altitude."

As a director, I had the privilege and responsibility of mentoring and training a group of Mary Kay consultants who had been recruited into the company, either by me or by one of my recruits. They were my "unit." I actually had one such negative person in my unit. Every year, the Mary Kay world "goes home" to Dallas for the extravaganza known as Seminar. We matched up members of my unit with members of other units to room together. This allowed them to build sisterhood and learn from each other. Every year, I had the challenge of finding a new group of three to room with this Eeyore because the poor souls she previously roomed with endured four days of black cloud negativity and vowed, "Never again!" She somehow managed to suck the life out of the shared room until the magic of the experience, that is Seminar, was left in ashes on the hotel room

Attitude Pass-Only Positive Vehicles May Proceed 51

floor. Each year she came to Seminar, I hoped against hope that she would hear something from someone else's mouth that would create a breakthrough moment for her attitude. Unfortunately, that never seemed to happen.

You see, my negative consultant was just like the Eeyores who would approach me after I spoke. They didn't really want a solution. They wanted to share their tar of negativity so that someone, *anyone*, would confirm and validate their position. If I had been a fly on the lapel of the directors who trained the classes my negative consultant took at Seminar, I probably would have heard her share her sincere belief that her director just didn't understand her unique obstacles and wasn't at all supportive of her career. Unfortunately, the negative people of the world gravitate toward other negative people and feed off each other.

Positive people attract positive people, and negative people attract negative people.

At a speaking engagement in Lansing, Michigan, I was in the conference hall before breakfast to check on the setup. While I was waiting for the event staff to join me, an older fellow walked by. I offered him my usual, "Good morning!"

"I don't know what's good about it, but it's morning," he responded.

I can't think of a more effective way to shut down a conversation. (Maybe that was his intention. Who knows?) I could have pushed the fact the sun was shining and both of us were still above ground and breathing, but I doubt it would have made a difference. He disappeared into the conference room across the hall.

A short time later the banquet manager, having concluded

our consultation, met up with this same fellow as he came out of his conference room.

"Is everything in your room satisfactory?" asked the banquet manager.

"As close as we're ever gonna get, I suppose," was the man's response as he walked away, leaving the banquet manager standing bewildered in the hallway. He looked at me for some sort of explanation although I had no connection to this cantankerous fellow.

"Take that as a 'yes' and run with it," I said with a smile. "Right," he said, and headed off in the opposite direction. I would bet chocolate (one of my most precious commodities) that the service I received from the hotel staff that day was far better than the service offered to the grouchy fellow across the hall.

It may surprise you to discover that positive people don't always wake up with a positive attitude. Some mornings, I wake up and say, "Good morning, God!" Other mornings, I wake up and say, "Oh good God, it's morning." But there is always a silver lining. If most of us took a serious look at our lives in comparison to others across the globe, we would see how very blessed we are. Generally, anything and everything in our daily lives beats a poke in the eye with a sharp stick!

Maintaining a positive attitude in our inherently negative world is not necessarily easy, which is why we need to be ever vigilant. A positive attitude is a choice. When we make it a daily choice, it becomes a habit.

I have developed some strategies that help me stay positive on a daily basis:

Never Compare

We all have our gifts. Each combination of human gifts is unique to that person. I have a gift for public speaking and decorating. For years, I desperately wanted to be a leading actress on Broadway. Truth be told, I didn't have the voice for it. I actually didn't have the voice for leading roles in *regional* theater, and I spent way too many years comparing myself to those actresses that consistently beat me out of those leading roles. (I *am* a heck of a character actress, but that is beside the point. And I'm pretty self-confident these days, if you haven't noticed!) Never compare yourself with anyone else. It's human nature, but when you do, I bet you always compare your weaknesses to their strengths. You lose every time you do that, so why would you do it? So long as I continued to compare myself to the ingénues and lyric sopranos, my self-esteem took hit after hit. It was not until I stepped away from theater completely that my true gifts were given room to shine, and my self-esteem grew and began working for me. I may go back at some point and do some community theater just for giggles. There are a lot more interesting character roles for women my age. If I do it, it will be just for fun and not because I need to prove anything to anyone -- especially myself.

As I travel, speak and train, I encounter other excellent trainers. I never compare myself to them. They each have their gifts and I have mine. I choose to compare myself only with my own best efforts, and then I strive to exceed those efforts. Never compare yourself with anyone else – only with your own best efforts and intentions.

Associate with Positive People

As I've said, positive people gravitate toward positive people, and negative people attract negative people. Make the choice to associate with positive people. I believe you will become like the five people you spend the most time around, so make sure they are positive people!

Here is a simple way to assess the people you spend the most time with. Make a list of the 10-15 people you spend the most time around. You're going to make a mark next to each person's name based on the following: when you leave their presence, do you feel energized, serene, enthusiastic, or better about yourself? If so, mark a plus ("+") sign next to their name. When you leave their company, do you feel drained, tired, on-edge, irritated or sucked dry? If so, give them a minus ("-") sign next to their name. If you feel nothing and are completely neutral when you leave their company, they get an equal ("=") sign. This list is for your benefit only and not for anyone else to see. This simple exercise separates the positive people in your life from the negative ones. Choose to associate with the positive ones. Consider negative people to be like toxic chemicals. You would not make a conscious decision to slip your hand into a vat of sulfuric acid. You would avoid doing so at all costs! Consider negative people toxic, corrosive and detrimental to your health. In your effort to maintain a positive attitude, such people are to be consciously avoided.

This is sometimes easier said than done and may not be something you can do overnight. Still, it is critical to maintaining your positive attitude. Slowly wean yourself from all your negative associations.

An office environment demands working with everyone, positive and negative. If there are negative co-workers at your office, limit your contact with them as much as you can. Have an honest exit line that works for you. Make sure it is honest. Never compromise your integrity even with little white lies. For the better part of

Attitude Pass-Only Positive Vehicles May Proceed

my life, my exit line has been, "Would you excuse me? I need to go to the bathroom." (For me, it's always true!) After completing my bio-break, I make a choice not to return to that group, person or conversation.

Sometimes, the negative people in our lives are our family. In that situation, wrap yourself in emotional Teflon. Just as sometimes it is necessary to come into limited contact with toxic chemicals such as sulfuric acid, you do so only when protected by special gloves or other protective gear. It's important to protect yourself as much as possible from emotional exposure to family members' negativity. You may need to double your diligence in the other self-protection tactics and make sure your self-talk is impeccable. If you consistently maintain a positive attitude in spite of negative family members, you may find yourself rubbing off on them instead of the other way around.

Grateful Journal

One of the most valuable tools at my disposal, with regard to maintaining a positive attitude, is a "grateful journal." Get yourself a simple spiral notebook -- it doesn't have to be fancy. Each night before you go to bed, take a moment to write down at least one thing you are grateful for. Every day you have something to be grateful for.

In my tumultuous life, I've had days where the best thing I've managed to come up with is, "Today, at the end of this horrible day, I'm grateful that I'm still alive."

Every day there is *something* to be grateful for. If you do this consistently and then look back at it after six to eight months, you will be amazed at how very blessed you are.

Positive Self-Talk

The most important factor in maintaining a positive attitude is positive self-talk. Speak only positive thoughts to yourself. Be nurturing and optimistic with your internal dialog. When a negative thought comes into your mind, cancel it out and replace it immediately with a positive thought instead.

Put these strategies to work for you and begin building the habit of a consistently positive attitude because your attitude does indeed determine your altitude.

Rest Stop
– Matters of Faith

Monday gave me the gift of love,
Tuesday peace came from above,
Wednesday told me to have more faith,
Thursday gave me a little more grace,
Friday told me to watch and pray,
Saturday told me just what to say,
Sunday gave me the power divine
To let my little light shine.

- Harry Dixon Loes

Before I started my walk with my Lord, The Colonel was the one "all knowing," "all powerful," being in my life. Even after I came to know and rely on an eternal wisdom, I always ran things by Dad to test my assumptions...just in case. Dad had no need for faith. To him, there was nothing his intellect couldn't work out. If his intellect happened to fail him, his sheer size and brawn would surely do the trick. Unfortunately, I have come to believe this was one of my father's greatest weaknesses.

When I was in junior high, we were stationed at Wright Patterson Air Force Base in Dayton, Ohio. In our neighborhood, we were surrounded on every side by Southern Baptists whose collective goal, it seemed, was to save the souls of the poor kids living in our home. My mother toyed with them mercilessly. A five foot carved reed "tiki god" decorated the front entry way of our home. It was surrounded by large potted plants and illuminated from the bottom with a spotlight. It was the mid-1970s and Mom dressed accordingly in psychedelic sarongs or tie-died caftans with her long hair pinned on top of her head with bones or chop sticks. Each time the neighborhood missionaries would come to the door, Mom espoused belief in Buddha, Baal, Hinduism, or some other equally mystical option, just to watch their reaction. Picture these well-meaning Baptist missionaries from the Bible-belt reacting to my mother, a drink in one hand and a cigarette in the other, all trussed up like a voodoo priestess and standing next to a pagan idol. I imagine they thought she was a demon of some sort! Even so, they were persistent. Every Sunday, they invited my sister and me to go to church with them. Every Wednesday, we were invited to a youth group function. I enjoyed going because it was an opportunity to get out of the house and to socialize and flirt with the cute boys – in truth, this was all that mattered to me. Each week, I asked for permission to go and Dad (being more pragmatic than Mom) would say, "I don't care if you go, just don't come home pumped full of b.s." Dad believed organized religion was just something invented by people who were too weak to handle reality on their own.

Mom's view on religion was a little different. I began to see a glimpse of it in the spring of 1974. We were still in Ohio, living in a town nestled between Dayton and Xenia called Beavercreek. On April 3rd, the storm to beat all storms dropped 148 tornadoes in 24 hours across 10 states. One of the hardest hit cities was Xenia. Among the 5,484 injuries caused by the storm, 1,150 were within Xenia alone. Of the 315 storm-related fatalities, 33 were from Xenia. It started in earnest around 4 p.m. with wind and rain and hail. I'd never experienced anything like it before,

Rest Stop-Matters of Faith

and I didn't know what to be afraid of. Having grown up in the Midwest, my mother had, and she was very afraid. When the hail stopped, the wind stopped almost completely and the sky turned a sickly greenish-yellow. My mother said, "We gotta get out of here – NOW." Our house was a ranch style with no basement and no crawl space. Suddenly, the wind came up again, and I looked outside to see our 1973 Chevy Blazer rocking back and forth on its tires, left to right. The pressure in the house made it impossible to open the front door, so Mom corralled us out the arcadia door and into the Blazer. We took off down the street, heading to a friend's house that had a basement. As we turned onto Dayton Xenia Road, my mother looked in her rearview mirror and said, "Holy ----! Kids, get down, away from the windows." Of course, I did not do as I was told. I looked to see what had scared her so badly, and there, coming down the road behind us, was the tornado my mother was trying to outrun.

Amid the panic, I noticed she was talking. "Dear St. Christopher, now we pray. Please protect us on our way. Dear St. Christopher, now we pray. Please protect us on our way." Over and over until we turned off the main road into our friend's driveway and were safely in their basement with them.

A couple hours later, we were given the "all clear." Rescue crews flooded into Xenia to help, and we headed home for the night. Around 10 p.m., Channel 7's weatherman, Gil Whitney, came on, frantically saying something to the effect of, "Oh my God, take cover Xenia. It's coming right over the top of you again." My mother grabbed a mattress and huddled us all in the bathtub. She covered us with the mattress as the rotation stormed over our house. There in the darkness, my mother prayed. This was surreal for me as I had never heard Mom pray before that day. Later I asked her about that day. Raised a Catholic, her reply was simply, "Old saints die hard."

From the moment my mother stepped away from her Catholic upbringing as a young adult, she has never, to my knowledge, had any need for formal religion. She does, however, have a very strong faith in a benevolent cosmic force. I learned this particular lesson – this road sign – from her: Faith matters.

Mom introduced me to the faith of "The Peaceful People," the Hopi Indians. (We have Hopi in our ancestry.) When I was very young, she shared the concept of Sipapu with me. Sipapu, it was believed by the ancient Anasazi Indians that inhabited the four corners region of the United States, is a small hole or portal from which all souls emerge and to which all souls return. Sipapu provides continuity to all life. This concept of continuity was very important to my mother. The ancient pueblo dwellers dug a small hole in the floor of their holy houses, known as kivas, to symbolize the one true Sipapu which is believed to be somewhere in either the Grand Canyon of north-central Arizona or Canyon De Chelly in the northeast corner of Arizona.

In Hopi tradition, Mom has always referred to the voice of God as a butterfly on her shoulder.

I was introduced to the concept of true faith – as compared to religion – when Mom began her recovery from alcoholism. I went with her to that very first A.A. meeting; I went to many of them actually. The second of the twelve steps is, "We came to believe that a Power greater than ourselves could restore us to sanity." That step is followed by making a decision to turn our life over to that Higher Power as we understand it. This was about FAITH, not about religion. While it seemed very cool at the time for a teenager to talk about being "higher powered," I slowly came to truly believe there was something bigger than myself, something bigger than my *dad*. That was a completely foreign concept in our household, and yet to me now it seems a

Rest Stop-Matters of Faith

very lonely and scary thought to imagine there is nothing bigger out there than my own, flawed, human mind.

During my last couple of years in college, I lived on campus. This gave me the freedom to fully indulge my eating disorder and brought me to a place and a moment during my senior year where I knew with complete certainty that if something bigger than me did not take over, I was going to die. I roamed the campus one day in a gray fog, finally wandering into the chapel at All Saints Newman Center.

As I look back, entering the chapel was highly unusual for me. "Church" had never been a welcoming place for me. Going to Mass with my grandmother was a painful exercise in obedience. We were told very clearly what to do, and what not to do, so as to not embarrass her. We dressed in the best clothes that Grandmother bought us and wore lace mantillas on our heads. We held them on with bobby pins lest they slip off and we offend God with our bare heads. I remember asking my Grandmother one time if the man at the front of the building (the priest) was God, and she slapped my face for being disrespectful. Even going to church with the Baptists in Ohio, I was always in fear. There was a great deal of preaching about hell and how we were all going there unless we were saved. I didn't know if I was saved or not. I was pretty sure it was the latter, and I was terribly afraid someone was going to stand up and point at me, calling me out as one of the terrible sinners that everyone was talking about. That's why I was always so relieved when the "churchy" stuff was over, and we could get down to the reason I was there: cookies, soda pop and boys.

That day, All Saints Chapel was completely empty – otherwise I would not have gone in. I sat down in the back pew and dropped to my knees. I didn't know if I believed in God. I didn't know how to talk to Him if He existed, or even how to quantify what was wrong or what I needed. Somehow, I just started talking as if I was talking to my dad because that seemed to make the most sense. I have no idea what I said, because that's not the side of the conversation I remember. That day was the first time (and there have been just a few) that I felt, without a doubt, that God spoke to me.

God and I had a conversation that afternoon. He metaphorically held me by my waistband over the quagmire that was my life and said, "I want to save your life today. I am eager, anxious, DYING to save your life today, but if we do this, we are going to do it My way. From here forward you are going to live clean, you are going to live sober, and you are going to live for Me. It's going to break My heart to throw you into that quicksand one more time, but if that's what it takes, that's what I'm going to do. The call is yours. What's it going to be?"

Because of that moment, I began in earnest to study the Bible, the Old Testament, the New Testament, the history of Christianity, the Dead Sea Scrolls – anything I could get my hands on. I began going to church on a regular basis. Some congregations I have enjoyed and others I have not. Be that as it may, I believe it's important to allocate time on a regular basis for your spiritual self – to fill your own tank. You can't give out of an empty tank; regularly attending whatever spiritual service speaks to you helps refill your tank.

In 1996, my husband received a job offer from a popular telecommunications company, Sprint, in Overland Park, Kansas. We were living in Phoenix, "The Valley of the Sun," and I was absolutely not interested in moving to the "cold and drafty Midwest." He turned it down. In 1997, a second offer came, again from Sprint in Overland Park. To get a feeling for the area, we decided to include Kansas City in the driving vacation we

Rest Stop-Matters of Faith

took that summer. I determined that if I absolutely had to, I could live there. The offer, however, was not sufficient to uproot our family and move across the country. In 1998, an inquiry came from Birch Telecom in Overland Park, Kansas. Again, it was an insufficient offer to justify the move although we were intrigued by the coincidence. Offers came again in 1999 and 2000. Now we were paying attention. We made jokes to each other, "Hey, maybe someone's trying to tell us we should move to Overland Park, Kansas..." Although the job offers dwindled at that point (the telecommunications industry was headed downhill in a barrel), we began spontaneously meeting people who had just moved to, or were vacationing in, Phoenix from Overland Park. We began seeing news articles about Overland Park with a frequency that astounded us.

In March 2002, it became surreal. In one week, we met four people from Overland Park, Kansas. We saw a news story on the front page of "The Arizona Republic" that mentioned Overland Park as having been voted the #1 place in America to raise your children by the National Chambers of Commerce. Nowhere in that article (on the front page of our local newspaper, no less) was any city in Arizona mentioned. Ron and I each read the article within an hour of each other at two different locations. That week there was a human interest piece on the late night news. The newscaster made a joke: "The city council in Overland Park, Kansas is working overtime..." (Apparently, public nudity was not illegal there and they were trying to get that changed.) The kicker was when a member of my Mary Kay unit, who was not privy to any of this, called me to share a dream she'd had that week. In her dream, the unit had earned the pink Cadillac and in the dream, the Caddie had Kansas plates. I said to Ron, "We gotta go. I don't think God could use a bigger stick to get our attention than He has this week. We've gotta go to Overland Park."

He said (steady and stable as he always is), "I'll put some feelers out and the next job offer that comes..."
I said, "No. The job offers have come and gone. We didn't heed them. Telecom is in the toilet right now. There won't be another job offer. Besides, when God called Abraham, Abraham did not say, 'What are the job prospects in Canaan?' He just went. We have to go on faith."

I tried to explain our need to move to my parents, one at a time. My father said, "If you want to go then go. Whatever your reasons are, I am sure they are valid. There is no need to bring God into this."

After explaining the phenomenon that brought us to this decision to my mother, she said, "Now that's a butterfly on your shoulder."

We set about arranging our lives financially so we could make the move without total financial ruin. Ron volunteered for a layoff he knew was coming – in essence, he quit his job. We packed up our lives, our kids, our whole existence for the past 23 years, and moved to Overland Park. Where we were going, we had no contacts and no relatives. We didn't know a soul in the city. I made a joke at the time that history would prove it to be the greatest leap of faith, or leap of folly – I wasn't sure which. I guess I expected that once we got ourselves here in obedience, the sky would open up and the blessings would rain down upon us. That's not exactly how it happened. Ron didn't immediately find a job here, and we struggled quite a bit for about 18 months. I tried to support our family on my Mary Kay business, while Ron delivered flowers by day and loaded trucks for UPS by night.

Years later, I can look back and see the blessings. My kids are happier and better adjusted here than they had ever been in Phoenix. Ron eventually found a great job with an excellent

Rest Stop-Matters of Faith

and stable company that values him and treats him with respect. Doors have opened here that led me to my speaking and training career, and I have discovered that I *love* the Heartland of America. None of that could have ever happened without that leap of faith in 2002.

I boldly declare my faith in God and rest my salvation in His Son, Jesus Christ. My faith is not the important message here, however. *Having* faith in something that is bigger than you is what is important. There are no strings attached to research. Go to the library and get books on faith. Educate yourself. Read the Bible. Read the Talmud and the Dead Sea Scrolls. Read the Koran. Read writings from Buddha and the Dalai Lama. Ask questions. Questions are free. Listen to the butterfly on your shoulder. I hope you will reach the same conclusion I did and seek the face of God.

Faith matters.

Fuel Station
– Prime the Pump

You've got to prime the pump
You must have faith and belief
You've got to give of yourself
Before you're worthy to receive
Drink all the water you can hold
Wash your face, cool your feet
But leave the bottle full for others
Thank you kindly, Desert Pete

- Billy Edd Wheeler

The Kingston Trio song, "*Desert Pete*," tells the story of a man, parched with thirst, traveling through the desert. He comes across a pump-style well with a bottle of water and a note from someone named Desert Pete. The note tells him he must not drink the water from the bottle, but use it to prime the pump so that water will flow from the well. Then, once he has had his fill, he must be sure to leave the bottle full, so the next person can also prime the pump and drink from the well.

Well I found that jar and I tell ya nothin' was ever prettier to my eye
And I was tempted strong to drink it, 'cause that pump looked mighty dry
But the note went on, "Have faith my friend, there's water down below.
You've got to give before you get – I'm the one who ought to know."
So I poured the jar and I started pumpin' and I heard a beautiful sound
Of water bubblin' and splashin' up outta that hole in the ground

I took off my shoes and I drunk my fill of that cool refreshing treat
I thank the Lord and I thank the pump and I thank old Desert Pete.

My father often quoted this song to me. "You've got to give of yourself before you're worthy to receive." The concept is simple, profound and fundamental.

Traveling with my family as a child was always an adventure. (Not always a good adventure, but always an adventure.) Because of Dad's mechanical abilities, our vehicles were always second hand, fixer-uppers, refurbished, redesigned or re-commissioned. (My first car was a rusted out red Fiat Spider Sport that Dad dropped a Volkswagen engine into. Of course, the Volkswagen engine sits differently in the engine compartment than a Fiat engine does, so Dad had to cut off, move and re-weld the motor mounts. After that, he had to reconfigure the camshaft and the flywheel, and, and, and...). Because of this mechanical "creativity," we were perpetually breaking down on the side of the road while traveling. Dad would pull out the tool box that contained the black electrical tape, duct tape, string, wire and every tool or gadget known to man. He would tinker and toy with it, get greasy up to his elbows, and somehow get the vehicle running well enough to limp into the next town where there was a garage for him to collaborate with to secure the repair.

Every now and then, the required repair was bigger than his emergency kit and skills could handle. A critical part or a weld was needed that duct tape couldn't fix. So we'd sit on the side of the road, waiting for a Good Samaritan to drive by and be willing to stop. When someone did stop, Dad would ask for a ride, and taking the faulty part with him, hitch a ride into town. Sometimes there was room for all of us, and we would leave the vehicle there on the side of the road. Dad would complete the repair in town, hitch a ride back out to the car, install the part,

Fuel Station-Prime the Pump

and drive back into town to pick us up. If there wasn't room for all of us, we would wait with the car until he returned with the necessary part. These days, such blind faith in people's kindness is unheard of. For Dad, and by extension for us, it always seemed to work out somehow.

For that same reason, long before cellular phones brought roadside assistance right to your car, my dad *always* stopped to help others. It didn't matter the location, where he was going, or how late he might be for an appointment. He stopped – every time. Even though I can't tell you how many times we received assistance, I can safely say we helped just as many others. Sometimes, he would get in there up to his elbows and, with his skills and his tools, solve the problem and the other person or family would be on their way. Sometimes we would be the ones offering the ride into town. Sometimes Dad and the stranded fellow would head off in our car, leaving Mom, Christi and me with the marooned family to keep them company. I don't ever remember questioning Dad's judgment in such situations. It was just who he was. I'm sure Mom had a few words with him about it throughout the years, but again, for Dad, it always seemed to work out.

One of these experiences stands out in my mind. We pulled over to help a family along the side of the road. They were Hispanic and spoke little English. (In the 1960s, that was quite a bit less common than it is now.) Early in their marriage, my folks had been stationed in Torrejon, Spain, so they possessed a fumbling command of Spanish. The stranded mother and father had three very small children and one on the way. I watched Dad communicate through a combination of broken Spanish, English and hand gestures. He pulled his magic tool box out, and working alongside the father, managed to fix the problem with their car. Relief flooded the mother's face and she started to cry. Each of the kids ran up and threw their arms around my father's knees. The father choked back tears and offered my dad a strong handshake saying over and over, "Vaya con Dios. Vaya con Dios." ("God be with you.") My father was visibly moved as we watched them drive off.

You never know when you will need help. Dad said that so many people had stopped to help him along his way that he was just paying it back. "You never know when you will be the one needing help, Lauren. Prime the pump and leave the bottle full for others."

I believe that the good my father sent into other people's lives more than primed the pump. He was not always gentle and not always easy to work with, yet he always had the best intentions for everyone.

One of Dad's life habits was employing young men to help him with his "project of the moment" and mentoring them. He had a wealth of stories about those who had taken him under their wing when he was young. Dad often told us the story of being five years old and meeting a grizzled old geezer who drove around the local ranch area gathering up scrap metal and other discarded items. The old man sold the metal to scrap dealers for a few bucks. He and my Dad became friends and Dad spent much of the summer with him, helping him load the scrap metal. He occasionally gave Dad a few coins for the help, but mostly Dad just enjoyed the friendship. He'd say, "I learned a lot from that old geezer. It was one of the best summers of my life."

Dad left school and home when he was thirteen. He was a massive, strapping fellow. Even at that young age, he struggled against the authority of his older sisters who tried their best to raise him while their father was on the road driving trucks. Out on his own at 13, he harvested alfalfa for a while with migrant crews, and he learned from them. He logged for a while in the pine stands of Idaho, and he learned from the logging crews as well. They played good-natured tricks on him and left the "grunt" work to him, but they also took care of him and gave him what they could – their knowledge and experience. After a year on his own, he decided he really didn't know any more than the "snot running out of my nose." He decided to go home and back to school. His father set him up to live with his Uncle Hasslet, who became a driving force in my father's life. Physically deformed and hardened by life as an outcast, Uncle Hasslet was not necessarily a kind man. Nonetheless, Dad was good for him and he was good for Dad. Much of the work ethic Dad instilled in us, he learned from Uncle Hasslet. Under Uncle Hasslet's tutelage, Dad graduated high school and went on to college on a football scholarship. Uncle Hasslet gave him what he had to give – a home and mentoring.

The gifts of time, attention and experience were given to him by others who took the time to mentor a hulking, headstrong, often belligerent teenage boy. These people "primed the pump and left the bottle full for others." Dad subsequently passed it on to other young men in kind. There was Wayne when we lived in Ohio; David up at the cabin in Durango; Manny in Albuquerque; and I'm sure a half-dozen or more I don't remember. For a short time, they would become a part of our family. They worked alongside my dad, ate with the family, and sometimes stayed with us to absorb Dad's experiences. I don't know what Dad paid them, although I'm sure he paid them something. Most important, he would take them under his wing and teach them. I suppose I could read into this habit his way to satisfying a longing for the son he never had, but it never detracted from his relationship with his daughters, so I leave it at that. We were learning as well – learning how to prime the pump.

Cell phones and safety issues often prevent stopping to help someone on the side of the road, but that doesn't mean we can't strive to do things for other people. The concept of giving to people is still valid, especially when it is without the expectation of getting something back. Priming the pump means that we give of ourselves out of kindness, rather than out of what we might get in return. In the 1980s, a popular bumper sticker read, "Practice random kindness and senseless acts of beauty." (That arose from a thought first penned by Anne Herbert, a Berkeley, California author.) It was not an original concept. It is based on the concept that what goes around comes around. Original thought or not, I loved that bumper sticker and the concept in general. Sometimes, when I'm driving through a toll booth, I'll pay for two cars and tell the cashier that it's for the car behind me. It gives me a giggle. Even simple things like helping someone older than I am lift their carry-on luggage into the overhead compartment will lift my spirits. It might mean giving up your seat on the subway or shuttle bus to someone that needs it more than you do. It might mean taking cookies or a plate of brownies to the bell ringer who is standing out in the cold gathering donations. It might mean shoveling your neighbor's driveway when you know they are out of town and will come home to a driveway full of snow and ice.

I was recently working and traveling in the United Kingdom. I had my train ticket and instructions to take the train to Manchester. From there, I was to go to my hotel in the village of Altrincham, which could be considered a suburb of Manchester. I took the smaller, commuter train to Altrincham and got off at the smallish, open air train stop (not really a station) in the pouring rain. At that point, I was a bit lost. Should I take a taxi? Could I walk to my hotel? Which direction should I set off in, dragging my luggage behind me? I was ardently looking at a map of the train system on the wall. No where on the map did

Fuel Station-Prime the Pump

it say, "Lauren, you are here, and you need to follow this route to get to your hotel," like I'd hoped. A man approached me and in a wonderful Welsh accent asked if he could be of assistance. I asked him if he was familiar with the hotel I was going to, and he said it was about a ten minute walk from the other side of the platform. He gave me very simple and easy-to-follow directions. I asked him if there was a lift to get up to the overhead walk that crossed the tracks to the other side of the platform. There was not, so he picked up my luggage and carried it up the stairs. I thanked him very much at the top of the stairs and told him I didn't want to be the reason he missed his train.

"I've got a good thirty minutes until my train and nothing else to do but help a lovely lady," he said as he picked up the luggage again. He carried it across the walkway and down the stairs on the other side. He told me to have a nice visit to Altrincham and was off back up the stairs to the other side of the platform. A random act of kindness I will always remember.

My husband is an excellent example for me in this area as well. He will always offer to help with someone's groceries, change a tire, hold a door open or offer a jacket to someone who might be cold. Some people might say he is just being an "old fashioned gentleman" and maybe he is, but it is deeply ingrained in him, and he never thinks of what he might get in return. He just does it. I admire him a great deal for that.

A wonderful series of commercials on television is currently promoting an investment or insurance firm. In the commercials, a person sees someone else offering a helping hand in passing without stopping for any thanks or recognition. That inspires the person to offer a helping hand to someone else, who is observed by yet another person who's then inspired, and the cycle continues. I *love* those commercials! I choose to believe it is not just the creativity of the advertiser, but that such things really do happen in cycles.

In the song "Desert Pete," the bottle full of water could have been a life saving gift. For that Hispanic family so many years ago, it could have been very serious for them to be stuck on the side of the road with the language barrier *and* a broken-down car to contend with. Still, it doesn't have to be something serious or lifesaving. Start small. Practice *small* random acts of kindness. In the grand scheme of things, your reward is the fact that you have primed the pump and left the bottle full for others.

Success Junction
– You Can Get There if
You Put Your Mind to It

"One of the greatest discoveries a man makes, one of his great surprises, is to find he can do what he was afraid he couldn't do."
– Henry Ford

On your life's journey, you will encounter basement people, and you will encounter balcony people. Basement people assume you *can't* do something, that you can't do anything. Balcony people believe that you *can* do anything if you believe you can and are willing to put in the effort.

I often call basement people the Eeyores of the world. That poor donkey has never had a good day in his life and is bound and determined that he never will.

Basement people are like crabs in a barrel. If you visit a seafood market where they sell live crabs, you'll notice there is usually no lid on the barrel. That's because if one crab tries to climb out, all the other crabs grab him and drag him back down into the barrel. That's what basement people do. They consistently endeavor, whether consciously or subconsciously, to drag others down.Basement people are most comfortable wallowing in groups of like-minded basement people.

Balcony people, on the other hand, rarely run in packs. Like Winnie the Pooh, balcony people are perpetual optimists. They see possibilities rather than limitations. Balcony people inspire and empower others to reach further and achieve more.

Let's say you decide out of the blue you want to climb Mount Everest. The basement people will say, "Are you crazy? You can't even walk three blocks to the market and you think you can climb Mt. Everest! Do you know how many people *die* on Mt. Everest every year? And they don't even bring the bodies down. It's too dangerous, so they just leave the bodies up there, frozen. The whole place is one big junk yard, littered with corpses and oxygen tanks. Are you *crazy*?"

On the other hand, share such a momentous goal with a balcony person and you are more likely to hear, "Everest!? Wow, that's exciting! It's a big goal. I know you can do it. What's your plan?"

A common paradigm among basement people goes something like this: "I will believe you can do it once I see you do it. I will trust you once you prove yourself trustworthy."

Balcony people come from a different paradigm. A balcony person believes in other people first. They say, "I believe in you. I believe you can do anything you set your mind to, and until you demonstrate otherwise, I am going to support you. Even when you fall short, I am going to continue believing in you until you believe in yourself as well." Balcony people *trust* people first until they prove themselves untrustworthy.

The first and most influential balcony person in my life was my father.

Dad came from small-town, potato-farming stock. He spoke often

Success Junction-You Can Get There if You Put Your Mind to It

of what he called "the small town syndrome," where everyone works in the field or the factory. Young kids got married and had kids of their own too young. While they dreamed of a life "away from here," they never got the chance to leave the small town. They went to work in the fields or the factories, often beside their parents, to support the kids they had too young and stayed right where they were. Their kids often found themselves married and pregnant too young and the cycle began again. Dad was the first one to tell me about the crabs in a barrel as he equated the crabs to his small town syndrome.

In elementary school, I wrote a report on "My Hero – My Dad." When I interviewed him, he told me the thing he was most proud of in his life was breaking away from the small town syndrome. When I consider all of my father's amazing accomplishments – including degrees in civil, mechanical and chemical engineering; lead design engineering on advanced composite airplane wings; a pioneer in wind energy farming; and more – it amazes me that he considered *that* to be his biggest accomplishment. He also said it made him very sad that he couldn't bring more of his family with him, that he couldn't instill in them enough belief in themselves to allow them to break the cycle as he had.

My father infused in my sister and me the belief that we could do anything we wanted to do if we were willing to work at it. We could achieve. We could become. My father believed wholeheartedly in the power of the human spirit.

I remember so clearly my father's enthusiasm and preparation on July 20, 1969. My parents set up the camera on a tripod to capture pictures of the television set and then gathered my sister and me so we could sit as a family and watch history happen -- the Apollo 11 lunar landing. There we sat, in the sunken living room, watching the fuzzy images on our black and white TV as "The Eagle" landed on the surface of the moon. I remember playing cards with my sister (frankly, a little bored) during the hours that followed the landing. With the nation, we waited for that unparalleled moment in time when man would actually walk on the moon.

As an Air Force officer, Dad felt a special connection with NASA. I don't know if he ever dreamed of being an astronaut, although his less-than-perfect eyesight would have prevented it. Nonetheless, he swelled with pride – as if it were his own accomplishment – when Neil Armstrong finally took that "one small step." He kept saying, "You see?! There is nothing you can't do. You can tell your children that in *your* lifetime we put a man on the moon. There is nothing you can't do."

Less than a year later, Apollo 13 took off from Kennedy Space Center carrying James Lovell, Fred Haise and Jack Swigert. About two days into the mission, the American public became aware there was a problem on board. Three American astronauts were in the void of space and there was a serious complication. An oxygen tank had exploded and blown out a large chunk of the command module. We watched, we waited, and we followed Walter Cronkite's updates. The crew could run out of oxygen before they reentered the atmosphere. The crew could run out of water. A toxic build-up of carbon dioxide could form. There might not be enough power to run the guidance system to get them back to earth. If they missed by a "hair's breadth," they would bounce off the earth's atmosphere and go hurtling into space. The command module may not power up again after being dormant in the frozen void for so many hours. After the explosion and the subsequent cold, the heat shield on the command module could be compromised which would cause the crew to be overcome and burn up in the reentry. So many potential catastrophes made it seem impossible for them

Success Junction-You Can Get There if You Put Your Mind to It

to come home alive.

I remember my mother pacing back and forth and saying, "That's it. We've lost three more. We lost three on the launch pad (referring to the Apollo 1 fire that took the lives of Gus Grissom, Ed White and Roger Chaffee) and now we've lost three more."

My father said, "No. We will get them back."

Mom ranted about the odds and cried in grief over lives already lost. Dad kept saying, "NO. We *will* get them back. This is America, damn it. The best American engineers are on this, and we will find a way to bring them back."

When the command module entered the earth's atmosphere on its return, there was a standard break in radio communications. I think it was expected to be about three minutes. To this eight-year-old little girl, it seemed like an eternity. My mother muttered and paced. My father stood stock-still – rooted to his spot in front of the television set – as if by sheer force of his will he could *make* it be alright.

When the sound of Commander Lovell's voice crackled over the airwaves, my father cried. Unabashedly, with tears freely flowing down his cheeks, he said, "You see, I knew we would bring them back. All it takes is ingenuity and willpower." (I think this was also the moment that solidified Dad's belief that duct tape can fix anything.)

In 1995, Ron Howard directed an amazing film recounting this particular mission. I watch it often. It's like comfort television for me. Each time the movie comes to the point that radio contact is broken, I find myself sitting on the edge of my seat. At the moment in the movie when the module splashes down,

I cry. It's foolish, I know. I know how the movie ends. I lived through it like so many Americans. I *know* how it ends, and yet I cry every time. Perhaps I cry because I so clearly remember my father's tears of joy and fulfilled faith in the human spirit.

Dad believed so profoundly that you can do anything you put your mind to. Anything you believe in and are willing to work for, you can do.

When I became a Sales Director with Mary Kay Cosmetics, my mentor was my National Sales Director Carolyn Ward, who has subsequently retired. Carolyn is a balcony person. Carolyn encouraged me in ways she will never know and perhaps never consciously intended. My years in Mary Kay taught me critical life lessons that will always be of benefit to me, and that is why I needed to travel that road for a while. Carolyn cared about my achievements and accomplishments within the organization, of course. More important, Carolyn cared about me and the total range of gifts I have been given. In large part, without even knowing it, Carolyn's encouragement eventually put me on the career path I now travel.

When someone achieves the position of Sales Director with Mary Kay, a celebration and a director's "debut" follows wherein the new director gives an address. My Senior Director, Jan Moses, encouraged me to send a video tape of my address to my National Sales Director. Because Jan suggested it, I thought it was something *everyone* did. Apparently not, because I received a note back from Carolyn (which I still have today) expressing to me what an amazing speaker I was, and how this inherent speaking ability would take me so far in life because so few people have it.

As a Director, I was consistently asked by other directors to speak

Success Junction-You Can Get There if You Put Your Mind to It

at events or at their unit meetings. I loved doing it and did so eagerly. I always assumed it was because I was new, or I was local, or I had achieved something that year. All of that may have been true. It also might have been because I was a really good speaker. I couldn't see that at the time.

During one summer's Seminar, I had the opportunity to spend twenty minutes alone with Carolyn in her suite. I had her all to myself. This was a very big deal because Carolyn was a mentor to *hundreds* of directors, and that much of Carolyn's time needed to be earned. I had achieved a ranking within the top twenty in the country that year for recruiting which netted me the one-on-one time. I'm sure she encouraged me to continue growing my unit and building my personal business and all the other things that would allow me to keep growing within the company. But what stands out in my mind was the other encouragement she gave me.

I had shared with her my vision of being on the big stage at Seminar and speaking as a top-three sales director or top-three national sales director. That was what I wanted more than anything else from my career at the time. Carolyn said, "Lauren, you can do this. You need to get behind that podium because Mary Kay *needs* you behind that podium. You will be one of the most inspiring and dynamic speakers to ever be recorded at Seminar. You can do it. I know you can. Now go do it."

A year or so later, I was struggling with an issue and called Carolyn for advice. The advice she gave me was not what I was looking for, and I argued with her. The conversation went nowhere from there and ended quickly. Afterward, I felt remorse at my behavior, and I wrote a note to Carolyn to apologize. She called me immediately upon receiving the note and said, "Before I address the subject of your note, let me say this. Lauren, you can write. Every note or letter I have ever received from you has not been written, but crafted. You write really well. You should write a book." Then we discussed the issue at hand and ended the conversation on a solid footing.

Without knowing it, Carolyn had encouraged me toward my current career path. She believed in me when I didn't believe in myself. Although that vision of being a top-three sales director or top-three national sales director speaking on the big stage at Seminar did not manifest itself, I do speak to crowds of a comparable size – teaching, training and (hopefully) inspiring people.

While there have been other very valuable mentors in my life, my dad and Carolyn were key in instilling in me the belief that I can do anything I want to do in this world if I want it badly enough and am willing to work at it.

You can do whatever you desire to do. Ask yourself, "What would I do if I knew I could not fail?" Create the vision. Establish a time frame and then set markers for yourself along the way. Share your vision and your goals with the balcony people in your life, and allow them to cheer you on. Not all goals come easily. Some take very hard work. Those who achieve are those who are willing to do that work. What action will you take *today* to move you closer to your goal?

Keep Driving
– *Then* You Can Relax

To everything (Turn, Turn, Turn)
There is a season (Turn, Turn, Turn)
And a time to every purpose, under Heaven
- Ecclesiastes (Adapted to music by Pete Seeger)

My father had a work ethic that was beyond compare. Dad was always working on something. For years, our freezer was filled with samples of advanced composite materials he was testing for some new airplane wing. He would sit at the table at night or on the weekends, watching TV and building prototype vertical axis wind turbines out of Pringles® cans. Some called him a workaholic (and he probably was!). Whether this is considered a good trait by all or not, he ingrained into his daughters this sound principle: Work *first* - then you can play later guilt-free.

I've tried very hard to instill this principle into my children. They are teenagers now, so it's still a foreign concept to them, but I think they'll get it. Work first – then you can play later guilt-free.

Please don't misunderstand. I don't believe in work, work, work, all the time. Dad also knew how to play like no one else. Indeed, he *played* as hard as he worked. He would arrive at the ski slope at the crack of dawn to make sure he hit the chair lift as soon as it opened, ski through lunch when the lift lines were shorter, and then ski like mad to get the last chair before the lift closed at the end of the day. (But he would always stop at the top of the mountain to take in the scenery.) No, I'm not an advocate of working all the time. I believe in doing what you *need* to do when you need to, so you can do what you want to do when you want to.

When we were children, my sister and I were not given an allowance. We were assigned chores based on our ages and capabilities.We were paid a small wage, or reward, for doing the chores around the house; screening litter boxes, cleaning bathrooms, helping Dad in the garage or helping Mom with the landscaping. Every day, and especially on the weekends, our chores had to be done BEFORE we could play. Once the tasks were done, we were free to do whatever we wanted. The wiser of the two children (my sister) learned quickly that if you just buckled down and did what you needed to do, you could get it out of the way quickly and be free for the rest of the day. It took longer for me to learn that lesson, and I remember many LONG days *pretending* to be working on what I was supposed to be doing. I would daydream and diddle at some creative avoidance to put off working on what I didn't want to do. Christi would rant and rave at me (as only big sisters can) about how it wasn't fair. She was working hard on her chores, and I was just messing around and wasting time! But she always got the last laugh. In no time at all, she would be done and off riding her bike and playing with her friends while I was stuck there, still a prisoner to my chores.

I remember one specific Saturday in Tempe, Arizona, when Christi and I were supposed to weed the front lawn. Mom had filled the front with beautiful landscaping; an "island" in the middle of the yard housed two large palm trees and lush bushes. Near the house were terraced levels of bougainvillea and other flowering bushes. In between, she had chosen a ground cover (not really a grass) called dichondra. It was like clover, only hardier and really beautiful. The only problem with this was keeping the neighbor's Bermuda grass from creeping in and taking over. Once or twice a month, Christi and I would spend a Saturday morning weeding the lawn to keep the Bermuda grass from taking root. On this particular Saturday, Christi stormed into the house after completing her half of the lawn and huffed, "Laurie isn't doing ANYTHING!" (She was right. I wasn't, although I wouldn't have admitted it at the time.) Dad came out front and issued the ultimate sentence. I would spend the rest of the day in my room. Furthermore (and this was the kicker), I would be back out here pulling weeds tomorrow while Christi went to see a movie WITHOUT me! I was absolutely mortified. Sunday afternoon movies were such a treat for us, especially because we were finally old enough to go on our own – just the two of us. That lesson affected me so much that to this day I remember the movie my sister got to see without me – it was the musical *Oliver*. (Afterward, to help make me feel better, Christi told me that it was no fun to go to the movies alone, and she would've rather I'd been there. I'm not at all sure that was true, but it did help a little.)

In 1967, my parents bought a piece of property in Colorado as a vacation investment. It was three acres of wooded paradise, and we spent every available weekend there. Initially, there was nothing but forest and meadows. We spent the next decade, as a family, building a haven. We slept in an orange six-man tent we called "the pumpkin" and began leveling land to build a cabin. Most people spend their leisure time relaxing. We worked every day. Certain tasks were slated for certain days; from clearing the "dead fall" trees and branches, and scraping old insulation from wall panels as the cabin went up, to painting, or gathering tinder and kindling for the fire pit. Every day, there was something to be done. Whatever it was, that something got done *before* we could relax and just enjoy being in the woods. Once the work was done for the day, it was time for "happy hour," and we would build a big fire, eat snacks and drink the cocktails or sodas that were reserved for those special occasions.

In 1976, my father retired from the Air Force, and he and I moved to Albuquerque where he went to work for the University of New Mexico. My sister and mom stayed in Ohio for a year, so Christi could finish her senior year of high school without transferring in the middle of the year. Dad and I were "a team" for a year. I was a teenager and still not fully buying into the "work first" concept. Every day, a list of things had to be done: homework, vacuum, dust, empty the dishwasher, laundry, etc. – the basics of running a household. I walked home from school and was expected to get started on the list. Many times Dad came home from work to find nothing had been done. He would rant, "What the hell have you been doing here for three hours?" I never had an adequate answer for him. I had been doing nothing. I remember it as a very difficult time for me because there seemed to always be a great black hole hovering over my shoulder. If I didn't get started on the list right away when I got home, the black hole would suck me in, and suddenly, three hours would be gone and Dad would be hollering at me. During that year, I really had to get a handle on the "work first" concept.

We were a team, Dad explained, like a football team. If the quarterback can't count on his offensive line to do their job *when* they need to do their job, then he's going to get sacked every time. The offensive line doesn't have the luxury of saying, "I know. I need to block for you. It's on the list. I'll get to it...eventually." The same goes for the defense. The defensive tackles can't say,

Keep Driving-Then You Can Relax   87

"Yeah, I see him. I'll get over there and bring him down at some point...get off my back about it." Every man on the team, he went on, needs to do what he needs to do when he needs to do it or the team falls apart. "If we are going to be a team, Laurie, I need you blocking for me. I need you blocking for me when you are *supposed* to be blocking for me, not in your own time and in your own way." That finally got through to me – that, and paying the consequences in school for not doing what I was supposed to do when I was supposed to do it. (Suffice it to say I was not a straight "A" student like my sister.) I discovered it is just easier to get what needs to be done out of the way first. Work first. Then you can play later guilt-free.

My husband has this same intrinsic work ethic. Perhaps it was his growing up on a dairy farm where the work has to get done whether you want to or not. The cows have to be milked when they need to be milked, whether you feel like it or not. For Ron, Saturday mornings are for work. He wakes up between 6:00 and 6:30 a.m. every day, naturally. On Saturdays, that means the laundry is started and the yard work is in full force early. Whatever needs to get done that day is usually done by 10:00 a.m. That gives him the rest of the day to relax and catch the obligatory power nap between 2:00 and 3:00 p.m. (like clockwork). Maybe he will start slow-smoking a brisket or catch a baseball game on TV. He is free to do whatever he feels like because the things that *needed* to get done are done.

As I said, my kids are teenagers at this writing. They are learning this lesson slowly, with a great deal of complaining and gnashing of teeth. As my daughter completes her degree at college, I'm seeing glimmers of the lesson learned. My son still has a way to go in the process, but he'll get it. We have instituted systems to help. Every day, we have a written list of things that need to get done. If it is merely verbalized, it is too easy to forget so we write it down. Everything on the list needs to be completed before any recreation can take place. There is *always* a list. We do this to develop work habits in the kids. If the lists were sporadic, there would be no habit building, so there is always a list. (My husband can be very creative in finding things that need to be done around the house.)

As adults, we sometimes feel like there is no end to what needs to be done. If you work first to get everything done before you play or allow yourself recreation, there will never be any recreation! I often feel overwhelmed with everything I have to do. Sometimes, there doesn't seem to be enough time in the day for all the tasks that need to be done. I write them down on a list and then prioritize them. I clarify what *must* be done immediately. Then, by establishing deadlines on the other items, I can determine stopping points where I can reward myself with entertainment. On Monday, I will do task A and task B. Once they are done, I can be done for the day. Task C and task D can wait until Tuesday. By maintaining this rolling priority list, I can get what I need to get done when it needs to get done and still give myself time for relaxing each day.

Work first. Then you can play later, guilt-free.

No Road Rage Allowed

"You catch more flies with honey than with vinegar."

— Mom

We have all heard this quote from the great universal sage, "Mom." Although, truth be told, I'm not sure how excited I would be about catching flies in honey – that sounds a little gross, frankly. The essence of the adage is this: it is important to be sweet like honey, not nasty like vinegar.

Mary Kay Ash often said that every human being on earth has an invisible sign hanging around their neck that says, "Make me feel important." I've found that to be so true.

I travel a great deal in my career. I've earned the moniker of "road warrior." While I was on the road recently, I trudged into a hotel lobby, weary and road-worn, totally ready to drop. I arrived at the same time as another woman who seemed to be just as ready for the day to end. Seeing her frustration, I stepped back and allowed her to check in first. I watched the exchange as her exhaustion and impatience sharpened the edges of her voice and snipped off the common courtesies that are, unfortunately, no longer common in today's society. She asked if breakfast was complimentary with her hotel points. The clerk told her it wasn't. She raised her voice and railed about how many nights she stays with this particular hotel chain and how breakfast is included at other chain hotels, and therefore, it should be included here as well. The clerk patiently explained that each hotel is free to offer whatever perks they choose at each level of the points tier. He told her she would find two complimentary bottles of water in her room, and a newspaper would be delivered in the morning. Muttering that she "doesn't even read the newspaper," she grabbed her room key and headed off to the elevators.

That left me alone in the lobby with the night clerk. I stepped up, and reading his name tag said, "Hello, Patrick. How are you this evening?" That simple courtesy gave him pause.

He took the time to glance up from his computer terminal and look me in the eye to see if I was sincere in my inquiry.

"Better than some, I guess," he replied. "How are you?"

"Ready for a soft bed," I said. "Do ya have any of those?"

He smiled then. "I think I can get you one of those."

As we continued the necessary paperwork to check-in, I said, "I have a few questions for you, Patrick. You let me know when you are ready for them."

"Fire away," he said.

"First – is breakfast complimentary with my hotel points?"

Bracing himself, he replied, "Not at this level, I'm afraid." (I knew that. I had just heard the other hotel guest grouse about it vocally, but I figured it never hurts to ask.)

"I understand. Second question – I am training tomorrow here at

No Road Rage Allowed

the hotel. Can you tell me which conference room I will be in?"

He did so.

"Finally, does the hotel have a hot tub?"

"No, we don't. Sorry."

I said, "That's not your fault, Patrick. I assume that there is a bathtub in my room that I can fill with hot water and improvise – right?"

His smile came back, and grew larger still. "I think I can do you one better than that, Mrs. Schieffer. How about we upgrade you to a hot-tub suite? At no charge, of course."

Then my smile got bigger. "That would be amazing. Thank you, Patrick."

The kicker on this whole exchange came when he handed me my room key along with a breakfast request card and said with a grin, "The hot-tub suite comes with a complimentary made-to-order breakfast delivered directly to your room. All you need to do is fill this out tonight and leave it on your door. They will bring your breakfast to your room at the time you have requested it."

Wow.

There was a time in my life that I might have assumed this upgrade happened because of my big brown eyes or my flirtatious eye lashes. Now I'm old enough to know that such an assumption would be optimistic at best. I know this upgrade happened because I was able to see the invisible sign hanging around Patrick's neck: "Make me feel important."

Mary Kay also said, "All that you send into the lives of others comes back into your own." While eloquently put, this concept is by no means unique to Mary Kay Ash. The concept of universal justice, the common belief that "what goes around comes around" is almost cliché. Still, I believe it to be true. Furthermore, I believe that whatever you send out is spiritually or cosmically magnified ten-fold and sent back to you. Boy, you want to make sure it's positive!

Over the years, as my children have grown through the surly pre-teen and teenage years, I've cheerfully provided ample embarrassment for them. It's not always "cool" to look people in the eye and smile at them, or even call them by name. I do it on a regular basis. I believe the sweetest sound to anyone's ears is the sound of their own name.

As I travel and train across the country, I experience a lot of hotel conference centers and meet a multitude of banquet staff. I make it a point to be courteous first. I offer my hand and introduce myself. I ask them their name if they haven't readily given it to me. I ask them if they are the person I will be working with throughout the day. (It is just more efficient to start with the person who can and will get things done.) If such is the case, then I let them know what adjustments I need made, what I need, and my priorities. Too often, the catering staff is bombarded by twelve different requests, and they head off to try to get them all accomplished without knowing which of the twelve are the highest priority. That sets them up to decide priorities on their own and potentially take grief if they prioritize incorrectly. For example, I tell them, "I need the boxes that have my training materials in them first. Then I need two extra table cloths." That way I can be doing what I need to do while they focus on getting the remainder of the requested items taken care of. Each time that the staff member completes a request, I thank them by name.

I do the same thing when I'm in a restaurant. I make a point to ask the server's name (if it is not apparent on a name badge of some sort). That way when they bring something to the table, I can thank them by name. If I need to catch their attention, I can call them by name. I don't have to wave or call "waiter" or "hey you" or (worst of all) snap my fingers. (Don't ever do that. It's just rude.) I don't need to do any sort of dance at all. I can simply call them by name. Again, the sweetest sound to anyone's ears is the sound of their own name.

One of my favorite habits, and one that causes my children much chagrin, is the habit of actually speaking to law enforcement officers. I love to pull up to an officer on a bicycle, the street, perhaps when they are stopped doing paperwork in a parking lot, or at a stoplight if there is enough time, and invite them to roll down their window. Unfortunately, the reality of American society today is that most cops will do so with trepidation. I often see them steeling themselves for an expected barrage of negativity.

Then I simply say, "Just in case no one has told you this week, we appreciate you and all that you do for us." It is so heartwarming to see the change come over the officer's faces.

Sometimes they say "thank you" hesitantly, waiting for the "punch line." Sometimes I get an open toothed grin and a chuckle. Their response doesn't really matter, though. What really matters is that I've taken the opportunity to share my gratitude with them. I know I'll someday be in a situation where I will need to be able to trust a member of law enforcement with my life. All that you send into the lives of others comes back into your own. I choose to send that trust, that gratitude, that positive vibe, out ahead of time.

I also do the same with sanitation workers. These people are seemingly invisible, and because they work in the refuse of our lives, it is all too easy to assume that they somehow have less value than anyone else. How often do you think the local garbage men get thanked for the smelly, dirty job they perform for our convenience? I think it's rare, if ever. So I take it upon myself. Yes, they get paid to pick up our garbage, but I can't imagine it's nearly enough to compensate for the filth and the smell. So when I see them on the street and it's appropriate to stop, I do so and let them know their efforts are appreciated.

Here in America, a simple, "How ya doing?" is not uncommon. What is uncommon is waiting for a response and actually empathetically listening to it. Empathy is so valuable in life. Not just any empathy, however, suits my bill. For empathy to work for you in the great cosmic turnaround, it needs to be a positive empathy. The world is chock full of Eeyores. We don't need any more.

Recently, I was training in downtown Atlanta. The partner I was traveling with was from the Atlanta area, and we were meeting a friend of hers for dinner. As we walked down the street toward our destination just before dusk, I made eye contact with a man passing in the opposite direction and smiled. "How are ya?" he said. "Great thanks. And you?" I replied. I don't remember his reply because my partner grabbed my elbow and increased her pace. She said, "Lauren, your 'Midwest, Little Miss Sunshine' routine doesn't fly here. Anyone making eye contact with you right now is a crack dealer." I know her heart was in the right place because it always is. I've thought about that encounter a great deal afterward and thought perhaps I should guard myself more often. I've subsequently decided against it. Given my history, it would be normal and natural for me to be guarded all the time. In that situation, the streets were well lit and still fairly heavily trafficked. I was not walking by myself, and my partner knew the area well. Yet guarding myself to the point that I don't make eye contact with or speak a kind word to *anyone* allows those who have done harm to me in the past to be in control of my attitude and my outlook. I absolutely refuse to do that. I am *never* foolhardy or foolish with my own safety. I simply choose to believe the best in people.

I believe this optimistic outlook is the reason I have so many friends and contacts in so many cities and industries. Any time I'm looking for input or advice, when I need expertise or a referral, I have a plethora of people to call upon. Sometimes I haven't been in contact with them for several years, but the relationship is solid because I've paved the way with kindness.

Whether it is the housekeeping staff in the hotels I stay in or the president of a consulting firm I deliver a keynote for, each person I meet has that invisible sign hanging around their neck that says, "Make me feel important." I try and see that sign on every person, not necessarily because it will come back to me at some point, although I think that is a good reason. More importantly, I do it because I know how it feels to be treated in a dismissive manner. I also know how it feels to be treated with respect and value. I choose the latter; therefore, I can do nothing less than be kind and treat each person with respect and value.

The cliché, "What goes around comes around," is true. All that you send into the lives of others *does* come back into your own. And Mom was right – you *do* catch more flies with honey. Therefore, make a point to look people in the eye and smile. Call them by name. Treat people with courtesy and kindness, respect and empathy. Go the extra mile to look past someone else's sharp words or impatience without returning in kind. Not only will you build a reputation as someone who is pleasant to be around and do business with, but you'll find it will begin coming back to you in ways you couldn't possibly imagine.

The Long and Winding Road

Many times I've been alone
And many times I've cried
Anyway you'll never know
The many ways I've tried
But still they lead me back
To the long winding road

- Paul McCartney

After reading my initial manuscript, my mother said I needed to decide what I really wanted this book to be. Is this supposed to be a self-help book? (Yes. We need more self-help books, don't we? Besides, I think a pool of wisdom is a good thing.) Is it a tribute to my father? (Yes, and hopefully it has shared his humanity as well.) Is it an autobiography? (No. That would be just boring.)

Whenever I travel and train, I endeavor to give my participants tools that they can use, specific "nuts and bolts" that they can put into practice immediately. (I've sat through enough "rah-rah" seminars myself to know that they are like Chinese food. While flavorful at the time, you are hungry for something substantial an hour later.) As I mentioned at the outset, each person's road is a unique and individual one. The road signs they notice along the way will also be particular to them, as will the impact they allow those road signs to have on their life.

In this book, I've shared with you a sampling of the road signs, also known as life lessons, which have had the most profound impact on the direction my life has taken. I've been forthcoming about when I've tripped up or ignored the signs along the way. I've discussed how I handled those circumstances, and strategies to implement that can help you in similar situations. I hope they've struck a chord with you, or helped you in some way. If they haven't yet, I hope they will. And as you run headlong into situations that are difficult to handle, glance back into these chapters. These summaries are an easy reference for reminding yourself why it is such a wonderful decision to choose the High Road:

Take the On-Ramp – Only Grounded Vehicles Permitted (Pillars of Serenity)

I believe the two Pillars of Serenity are the legs upon which we live meaningful, productive lives. They are both equally important. You can't embark on any journey (especially not one onto the High Road) until you have your own self-esteem in place. Know where your value lies – which is in your very existence. Knowing in your core that you have value, that you are fearfully and wonderfully made, allows you to make the choice to treat all people with respect (whether or not you like what they think, say, or do). The first pillar is critical to the second because you can't treat other people with respect if you don't respect yourself. Again, let me reiterate that I'm not asking you to respect all people. I've met people on my journey I simply can't respect. I'm asking you to *treat* all people with respect.

The second pillar is reciprocally critical to the first. If you aren't treating others with respect, at some level (even if it is subconscious) guilt will seep in and rob you of your self-esteem. These two pillars function for you in the background like the operating system on your computer. They are the operating system for your psyche. Without these two Pillars of Serenity, nothing else functions properly.

Detour – Take the High Road

Stepping up onto the High Road of Principle is a choice we make every day. Some days it seems harder than others. Some days walking the High Road isn't very much fun, but it's always the right thing to do and the most powerful road to be on. When you are on the High Road, you don't have to question your intentions. There is not a small, nagging guilt from knowing you should have done something that was more principled. Walking the High Road is about living the words of Mahatma Gandhi, "We must *be* the change we wish to see happen in the world." It is leading by example and being the bigger person. Someone has to be. It might as well be you.

Fork in the Road
– Keep Right to Choose Response

There is a profound difference between reaction and response. Reaction comes from the gut. It is instinctual and emotional. Response requires thought. I've found that response is always the better choice. The simple truth that was shared with me in treatment speaks volumes: "What happens to you in your life is not as important as how you choose to *respond* to what happens to you in your life." Regardless of what may have happened to you, choose response. Don't give anyone else control over your emotional serenity and stability.

Welcome! You're Here by Choice

For every choice, there is a result. Good results come from good choices, and bad results come from bad choices. Don't spend time dwelling on bad choices you have made. Trust me, we all make bad choices. The most important factor is to learn from those bad choices and atone for them when necessary. That way we can make better choices next time. Focus on the good choices you have made and how you can continue to make those good choices.

Fabrications Ahead
– Tell the Truth, It's Always Easier

When you tell a falsehood – a lie of any size – you are then sucked into the perpetual hamster wheel of having to remember the lie and whom you told it to. That causes even your strongest supporters and best of friends to always have a nagging cynicism about anything and everything that comes out of your mouth. Telling the truth is just easier. It is less stressful. It requires less "gray matter." And it eventually builds for you a reputation as someone who is trustworthy and truthful in all situations.

Caution! Uncomfortable Shoes Ahead

I've found in my life's journey that there are three sides to every story: yours, mine and the truth. Consistently trying to place yourself in another person's shoes and walking around for a while enables you to see any situation from a different perspective. You can't empathize with someone until you have taken those potentially uncomfortable steps, and without empathy it is impossible to find any common ground. Ask yourself, "What can we agree on?" Until you have walked a mile in their moccasins, true and honest communication will never happen.

Attitude Pass
– Only Positive Vehicles May Proceed

I truly believe a positive attitude is the single most important factor in any individual's success. I've never met, nor heard of, anyone who is wildly successful in life with a consistently negative attitude. You can do everything wrong with the right attitude and still succeed. You can do everything by the letter with a bad attitude and still go nowhere in life.

Maintaining a positive attitude in an inherently negative world is a choice that has to be made every day. When you make that choice consistently, it becomes a habit. When you maintain that habit consistently, it eventually becomes a personality characteristic. Endeavor to see the silver lining in every situation. Assume the best of everyone and keep a smile in your heart because your attitude determines your altitude!

Rest Stop – Matters of Faith

To believe we are alone in this massive universe is a very lonely and scary mindset. Believe in and have faith in something bigger than yourself. There are no strings attached to research. Ask questions. Questions are free. Seek out your Higher Power and find out what He has to say to you. Find something bigger than yourself that you can believe in and begin turning things over. Doing so allows you to release those things not in your control and focus on what is in your control.

Fuel Station – Prime the Pump

You have to give before you get. Practicing random kindness was not a new concept in the 1980s when the bumper sticker was created. The concept of "what goes around comes around" is centuries old. When you prime the pump – when you practice random kindness – what you get back is priceless. You get back the satisfaction of having done it. It is never a tit-for-tat. I believe in the grand cosmic cycle that you get it back at some point – just as I did that day at the train station in Altrincham, UK. *"You've got to give of yourself before you're worthy to receive... (and) leave the bottle full for others..."*

Success Junction – You Can Get There if You Put Your Mind to It

The most important factor to achieving what you want in this world is the belief that you *can*. Second is the willingness to work for it. It is also critical to surround yourself with balcony people who believe in you. Determine who the balcony people are in your life, as compared to the basement people. I'm not saying you have to shut off, be rude to, or abandon the basement people in your life. After all, you may be the only balcony person in *their* life! Simply don't allow them to influence your consciousness or your serenity.

Establish goals for yourself and then set a specific plan for achieving them. Share those goals with the balcony people in your life and keep plugging at them. Think of all the amazing hardship-to-success stories out there: Thomas Edison, Helen Keller, Michael Jordan, Abraham Lincoln, Ronald Reagan, and hundreds of others. If you want something badly enough and are willing to work to achieve it, you *can* do anything you set your mind to.

Keep Driving – Then You Can Relax

Doing what you *need* to do when you need to do it allows you to do what you *want* to do when you want to do it. The classic fable of the ant and the grasshopper illustrates this so well. The ant works throughout the summer, gathering what will be needed to survive the winter. In the winter months, the ant can snuggle and relax, cozy in the ant hill with plenty to eat until spring. Meanwhile the grasshopper plays and lounges in the sun, asking, "Why bother about winter now?" Of course he learns this lesson in a very dramatic way as he slowly starves to death in the winter.

There will always be work that needs to be done. Learning to prioritize and doing what needs to be done up front allows you to relax when it is completed and not be weighed down by guilt over what still needs to be done.

Just like the football team analogy my father gave me so many years ago: Each member of the team has a job to do *at a certain time*. Doing the job when the job needs doing is what makes the team work.

That way, when it comes time to relax or play, you can do so with a free conscience and a light spirit. Putting your priorities in order allows you to relax when the time comes.

No Road Rage Allowed

As Mary Kay Ash is often quoted, "All that you send into the lives of others comes back into your own." I want to make sure it is always positive. It doesn't cost anything to be nice to people, to call them by name, to smile at them and offer courteous conversation. It costs nothing to treat everyone with dignity and respect. The gift you get back is intangible and priceless, like a great cosmic boomerang. Being nice to people makes a difference. It enriches both your life and theirs.

Each person's road is unique, as is their path up to the High Road. I would love for this book to offer an initial compass setting to those looking for a route onto that High Road. Because our paths are particular to ourselves, I can't give you a specific roadmap. Even though I can't give you a guaranteed GPS with turn by turn instructions (in 500 ft, exit right to the High Road...), I hope these pages have pointed you in the right direction. Happy traveling and I'll see you on the High Road!

About the Author

With a B.A. from Arizona State University, Lauren Ann Schieffer has risen to management in every company she has worked for. During her fast-moving career, she rose from a receptionist at a moving company to sales director of a major cosmetics company thanks to her relentless drive and her refusal to set limits on herself. She then forged those experiences into a successful career as a highly sought-after public speaker. Lauren's passion is motivating people to shake off mediocrity and excel while remaining positive and successful in today's workplace.

Lauren and her family live in Olathe, Kansas.